Negotiating the Freedom of Namibia

Hans-Joachim Vergau

Negotiating the Freedom of Namibia

The diplomatic achievement of the Western Contact Group

Basler Afrika Bibliographien 2010

Published by
Basler Afrika Bibliographien
P.O.Box 2037
CH 4001 Basel
Switzerland
www.baslerafrika.ch

Originally published 2006 in German by Nomos Verlagsgesellschaft: "Verhandeln um die Freiheit Namibias. Das diplomatische Werk der westlichen Kontaktgruppe". Völkerrecht und Außenpolitik 73.
Translated by David R. Ward MBE.

For the translation the authors gratefully acknowledge the support of the Archives of the Anti-Colonial Resistance and the Liberation Struggle (AACRLS), Windhoek.

Graphic design by Petra Kerckhoff, Basel.
Printed by Lightning Source UK Ltd., Milton Keynes.

ISBN 978-3-905758-17-7

Contents

List of abbreviations

AG	Administrator–General
AKTUR	*Aksiefront vir die Behoud van die Turnhalle-Beginsels* (Action Front for the Retention of Turnhalle Principles)
CAA	Central Administrative Authority
CAN	Canada
CG	Contact Group of the five western nations (CAN,D,F,GB,USA) which conducted negotiations on Namibia from 1977 to 1990.
CSCE	Conference on Security and Co-operation in Europe
D	Federal Republic of Germany
DB	*Drahtbericht* (reporting telegram) = official telegram from a German mission abroad to the Federal Ministry of Foreign Affairs in Bonn
DE	*Drahterlaß* (telegraphic instruction) = telegram containing instructions from the Federal Ministry of Foreign Affairs to one ormore German missions abroad
DGVN	*Deutsche Gesellschaft für die Vereinten Nationen* (German United Nations Society)
DMZ	Demilitarised Zone
DTA	Democratic Turnhalle Alliance
ECOSOC	Economic and Social Council of the United Nations
F	France
FAZ	*Frankfurter Allgemeine Zeitung*
FLS	Front-Line States (Angola, Botswana, Zambia, Tanzania,Mozambique, and from1980 also Zimbabwe)
FM	Foreign Minister
GA	General Assembly of the United Nations

GB	Great Britain
ICJ	International Court of Justice in The Hague/Netherlands
IG	*Interessengemeinschaft Deutschsprachiger Südwester*(Community of Interests of German-speaking South-Westers)
MPLA	*Movimento Popular de Libertacão de Angola* (Popular Movement for the Liberation of Angola)
NATO	North Atlantic Treaty Organization
NY	New York
OAU	Organization of African Unity
PIM	Pre-implementation Meeting (UN Conference in Geneva 1981)
PM	Prime Minister
Quintet	The unchanging CG team 1977/78 (Paul Lapointe/CAN, Don McHenry/USA, James Murray/GB, Albert Thabault/F, Hans-Joachim Vergau/D)
RL 320	Head of Section 320 at the Federal Ministry of Foreign Affairs Bonn (responsible i.a. for Namibia, RSA and the FLS); this designation in the text refers exclusively to the *author* who held this position from 1980 to 1985.
RSA	Republic of South Africa
SC	Security Council of the United Nations
SCR	Security Council Resolution, e.g. SCR 435
SG	Secretary-General of the United Nations (Kurt Waldheim 1972-1981, Javier Pérez de Cuéllar 1982-1991)
SGA	Special General Assembly of the United Nations
SU	Soviet Union
SWAPF	South West Africa Police Force
SWAPO	South West Africa People's Organization of Namibia
SWATF	South West Africa Territory Force
UDI	Unilateral Declaration of Independence (Rhodesia)
UN	United Nations

UNITA   *União Nacional para a Independência Total de Angola* (National Union for the Total Independence of Angola, Opposition Movement led by Jonas Savimbi)

UNSR   United National Special Representative (Martti Ahtisaari)

UNTAG   United Nations Transition Assistance Group

USG   Under-Secretary General

ZANU/PF Zimbabwe African National Union/Patriotic Front

ZAPU   Zimbabwe African People's Union

ZEI   *Zentrum für Europäische Integrationsforschung,* Bonn (Center for European Integration Studies, Bonn)

Foreword

At the beginning of 1977, several members of the United Nations Security Council prepared a joint initiative in order to resolve the deadlock over South Africa's illegal occupation of Namibia. In this study, the multi-facetted political and diplomatic developments – and dramatic setbacks – are analysed by a key participant in the emerging negotiations.

Hans-Joachim Vergau at the time was a highranking German diplomat and West Germany's representative to the UN Security Council's Western Contact Group throughout the entire negotiation process. Many initiatives to keep the process going were undertaken as a result of his activities, especially during the difficult times of the Reagan Administration when serious obstacles were placed in its path.

His book, which was originally published under the title *Verhandeln um die Freiheit Namibias. Das diplomatische Werk der westlichen Kontaktgruppe*[1] deals with some major achievements which should be mentioned here.

The South African strategy to avoid both Namibian independence and sanctions by the UN Security Council relied on the assumption that SWAPO, the only Namibian liberation movement officially recognised by the UN, would be very resistant to Western plans to keep its PLAN soldiers out of Namibia during the elections and the presence of the South African army inside Namibia. The other stumbling block was the status of Walvis Bay. These were very difficult issues for SWAPO because the movement had many reasons to distrust the whole diplomatic process. The main reason, as Dr Vergau clearly states, was that the Foreign Ministers of the Western powers were not seriously prepared to use the instrument of sanctions against South Africa, not even after the Cassinga massacre.

---

[1]   In: Völkerrecht und Aussenpolitik, vol 73, 2006, Baden–Baden (Nomos),

SWAPO had to avoid the risk of losing its claim to be the sole representative actor in Namibia, which was the basis of its international standing and relevant for international support. As such, the organisation had to tread very carefully, even if the diplomats became impatient. It is very interesting to note how important the advice of the Liberation Committee of the OAU was, especially through Julius Nyerere of Tanzania and Olusegun Obasanjo of Nigeria, in order to influence SWAPO to take that risk. This included the constitutional concept of a multi-party system and other core constitutional rights governing legal procedures and property rights *inter alia*.

Germany's contribution through Foreign Minister Genscher was to keep the UN Resolution 435 of 1978 which provided a framework for Namibia's independence, on the agenda for many years during the Reagan Administration, which demanded a linkage between Namibian independence and the withdrawal of the Cuban troops from Angola, despite US support for the Angolan military movement UNITA. The time was used to get German Namibians into contact with SWAPO and keep channels open between SWAPO and the South African Government.

However, time was working against the apartheid regime. The internal struggle in South Africa weakened the apartheid system. South African troops were challenged by the Cubans in Angola, and international political change initiated by Gorbachev opened the gate for independence because of the Soviet-US agreements to minimise global tensions. It also spelled ideological disaster for the apartheid regime because Pretoria could no longer use the threat of Communism as a pretext to defend its colonial rule in Namibia.

Dr Vergau describes how the process encountered obstacles even in the last few months prior to the 1989 independence elections in Namibia. UNTAG forces of the United Nations who were to oversee the independence process were delayed in northern Namibia. SWAPO tried to establish bases for its troops within Namibia. The presence of PLAN soldiers in the country, who obviously hoped to be granted protection by UNTAG, was used as a pretext for a massacre by the South African army. The diplomats, including Vergau, had no reliable information about that sad event, which will be an issue for future historians in Namibia. International efforts made it possible to manage the crisis.

This book gives a precise view of the long diplomatic struggle to achieve Namibia's independence through UN activities from the perspective of one of Germany's most influential diplomats. Hans-Joachim Vergau's commitment to the cause of independence bridged dangerous periods, including those where the Western powers and even his superiors did not apply the necessary pressure on South Africa until the apartheid regime itself had started to crumble.

Given the importance of Dr Vergau's study, the German/Swiss Country Committee in support of the Archives of Anti-Colonial Resistance and Liberation Struggle project based at the National Archives of Namibia in Windhoek, initiated this English version of the original study, as such making it accessible to a wider and also Namibian readership.

Prof. Dr. Helmut Bley
Hannover, May 2010

Introduction

At the beginning of 1977, five members of the Security Council caused quite a stir at the United Nations in New York. The Five were the permanent members of the Security Council, France, Great Britain and the USA, plus two non-permanent members elected in addition from 1 January, namely Canada and the Federal Republic of Germany. These Five set about turning the tide in a debate which had been raging for years over problems in Southern Africa, principally apartheid, Rhodesia and Namibia, by preparing a joint action initiative to resolve the issue of Namibia. Joint action among a group of Security Council (SC) members was nothing new. But the fact that South Africa's most important remaining international partners actively joined forces did indeed cause a stir. It gave rise to the hope that they might finally shift the apartheid regime in Pretoria, which had previously blocked all progress, towards an internationally acceptable position which respected human rights.

The Namibia Initiative of the Western Five achieved its objective in 1990: an end to the fighting, South Africa's withdrawal and Namibia's independence with a democratic constitution based on the rule of law. This multi-facetted political process, which repeatedly experienced dramatic setbacks as well as hard-won progress, is a core component of the new state's genesis. The people of Namibia thus naturally have a legitimate right to be fully informed about this process. It is also a timeless lesson for all students and practitioners of international negotiating, which has a wealth of stimulating and creative dimensions.

The Namibia negotiations have already been documented several times. But all these publications, even those of respectable quality, have had to rely almost entirely on published material and interviews.[1]

---

[1]   All loc. cit.: Brenke; Jabri; Melber, in "Conflict Mediation …"; Engel/Schleicher,

1

The author of this publication can draw on a considerably broader range of sources. He has borne virtually constant witness to the negotiating process and was directly involved in the initiative of the Five. From 1976 to 1980 he was desk officer for Namibia at Germany's UN Mission in New York and subsequently, until 1985, Head of the Section (320) which dealt with Namibia at the Federal Ministry of Foreign Affairs. Following an intermediate posting to Paris as Minister, he returned to New York as deputy head of the UN Mission with the rank of Ambassador from 1987 to1993, participating personally once again in all aspects concerning Namibia. The author therefore has access to comprehensive source material, which arose during the process and is thus authentic.

The purpose of this publication is to present and evaluate what really happened in the course of diplomatic developments from 1977 to 1990. It largely excludes Namibia's prior history and treatment at international level[2] as well as the peacekeeping operation undertaken by the United Nations Transition Assistance Group (UNTAG)[3] in 1989/90 to implement the settlement plan.

---

pp.259-336; Wenzel, pp.117-123. Namibia's total population (according to Federal Ministry of Foreign Affairs country profile): 1977: 758.900 inhabitants (of which 357,000 "Ovambos"; approx. 90,000 "Whites", of which approx. 23,000 of German origin, of whom about 6,000 were German citizens). 1990: 1,294,000 inhabitants (of which 641,000 "Ovambos"; approx. 103,500 "Whites", of which approx. 25,000 of German origin, of whom about 15,000 were German citizens). For 2005 the Namibian Embassy in Berlin puts the country's total population at 1,900,000.

[2]   For the history up to 1977 see loc.cit.: Eckart Klein, pp.485-490; Steltzer; Jaenecke, pp.186-203; Brenke, pp.7-19; ICJ Advisory Opinion 1971.

[3]   United Nations: The Blue Helmets, loc. cit.pp.203-229; Ahtisaari and Prem Chand in Weiland/Graham loc. cit.

2

A The 1977/78 negotiations up to the settlement plan in accordance with SCR 435

I The founding and mandate of the Contact Group

The SC had unanimously adopted the following in the operative paragraph 7 of Resolution 385 on 30 January 1976:

> Declares that in order that the people of Namibia be enabled to freely determine their own future, it is imperative that free elections under the supervision and control of the United Nations be held for the whole of Namibia as one political entity.

Paragraph 8 sets out the detailed arrangements for UN supervision through the SC, an initial definition of the remit for the later UNTAG.

The Resolution responded to constant demands from the UN General Assembly (GA) and was unanimously welcomed there by the Western delegates.

Faced with a new constellation at the beginning of 1977, the Africans were now dealing with such a high-calibre western group in the SC that they decided to take these Five at their word with their applause for SCR 385 and force them to show their true colours openly at the UN by drafting tough Resolutions aimed at South Africa, which also included sanctions under Chapter VII of the Charter. They swiftly prepared four draft Resolutions to this end and called for a debate to commence on 21 March. The first draft, which demanded the immediate abolition of the apartheid system, was acceptable to the West. The second draft focused on measures against South Africa under Chapter VII in the event that South Africa did not immediately halt its illegal behaviour "in South Africa and in Southern Africa as a whole", which included Namibia. A particularly compelling reference to Chapter VII came from the new formulation that

South Africa was in a "state of war" against the UN due to its military occupation of Namibia. The third Resolution sought a strict embargo on arms supplies and nuclear co-operation. The fourth Resolution strongly recommended the cessation of all foreign investment in and loans to South Africa.[4]

The competent experts of the Five in New York had met several times since January for informal consultations on developments concerning the SC. This was a natural, almost automatic practice in a UN context between partners with similar interests. The same also applies of course to the heads of the UN missions. There was a considerable need for action because drafts 2 and 3 at least were regarded as unacceptable at the time whereas the Five – especially in the light of SCR 385 - wanted to avoid a veto or no-vote at all cost. In one of these consultations on 4 March 1977, the US participant suggested that the Africans might be persuaded to withdraw the controversial Resolutions by an SC Consensus Statement. If such a statement imposed tough and convincingly argued demands on South Africa, more could be achieved – also from the Africans' point of view – than with drafts which would fail in the SC. In talks between the five Heads of Mission and their experts at the residence of the German UN Ambassador, Rüdiger von Wechmar, on 9 March it was indeed decided to work towards such a "statement of principles".

Participants at the same talks also discussed the unfavourable state-of-affairs that the West was continually merely reacting (mostly negatively) in the UN to African initiatives instead of taking the initiative themselves in a specific area, e.g. the Namibia question. The following had led to this approach:

Back in January 1977, the head of the UN section in Bonn, Helmut Redies, had complained to the German UN Mission in a long-distance call

---

[4] The 4 texts were distributed as drafts (in blue text) on 29.3.1977 under SC documentation numbers S/12309-12312.

about the Federal Republic of Germany being condemned by name in GA Resolutions for cooperating with South Africa, which the Federal Government found extremely disturbing. He suggested that it might be better to take a proactive role in a specific area instead of adopting a permanent defensive strategy. In view of the current presence of five NATO countries in the SC, the best thing would be "to attend to Namibia on the basis of SCR 385".

When Redies came to New York on 28 February after consultations at the State Department, he reported that Gerry Helman, the leading US expert in his opinion, as well as Donald Petterson and Assistant Secretary of State for African Affairs, William Edmondson, shared his support for starting "something on Namibia" independently as the Group of Five in view of the favourable constellation in the SC. However, there was still no approval from on high: policy on Southern Africa was determined by President Jimmy Carter in consultation with Secretary of State Cyrus Vance and the National Security Council. Initially, they still considered holding a "Namibia Conference" with UN participation in line with an earlier Kissinger proposal.[5] But UN Ambassador Andrew Young was now instructed informally to ascertain the opinions of the other Four, individually and in strict confidence.[6]

---

[5]   For more on the talks between the Five on 9 March 1977 cf. reporting telegram DB 423 of 9.3.977 from New York. For the Kissinger Concept cf. DB 2646 of 20.10.1976 from NY and DB 368 of 20.10.1976 from Pretoria. Also Vance loc. cit. pp.272-274. Vance was referring solely to this concept when he mentioned a suggestion by the American UN Ambassador Andrew Young on cooperation between the Five back in January 1977. In his portrayal of the CG's actual Namibia Initiative, Don McHenry (from 1977 until the beginning of 1981) rightly features as the main US protagonist and Young only in the margins. Vance's generally helpful contribution suffers from his tendency to view the other Four as bit-players in a US advance; he incorrectly states that the USA chaired the later CG. (Cyrus Vance, loc. cit. pp. 276 to 311). The American Henry Miller was McHenry's commendable constant assistant in Namibian affairs.

[6]   DB 349 of 28.2.1977 from NY (Redies did not include the strictly confidential information in the DB with wide distribution and only passed it on to FM Genscher in Bonn).

On the morning of 1 March 1977, Redies was the first to be asked by Young at the UN building – in the presence of the author – how Germany would respond to the idea – not yet approved by the White House – to task the Five, in the event of a satisfactory outcome to the SC debate, with first undertaking a *démarche* by their Ambassadors in South Africa and then, depending on the result, instituting negotiations on Namibia. Redies declared without hesitation that he presumed the German side would welcome such a concept and that he had already indicated this at the State Department the previous day.[7]

The constellation in the SC at the time and the course of events described here suggest that the idea of such an attempt "was in the air" in those days; an option of this kind was presumably also being considered in London, Paris and Ottawa at the same time.

On 14 March, FM Hans-Dietrich Genscher was in Washington for consultations, and von Wechmar briefed him on the current status of both the SC debate and the US soundings on Namibia. The Minister, who had already been updated on Namibia by Redies, decided that we should actively participate in both the action in the SC aimed at a "statement of principles" as well as in an initiative of the Five on Namibia. At the same time, he instructed us to ensure that the Namibia Initiative was launched, even if the SC debate resulted in an unsatisfactory outcome.[8]

The Five had arranged to hold their next round of talks at the Canadian UN Mission on Wednesday, 16 March 1977.[9] While fresh attempts to reach agreement with the Africans were constantly being made, this is where the group met over the next several weeks to discuss the situation in the SC and the "statement of principles". For the first time, however, they had the additional task of elaborating a very specific concept to launch

---

[7]   DB 359 of 1.3.1977 from NY.

[8]   DB 464 of 14.3.1977 from NY.

[9]   DB 482 of 16.3.1977 from NY.

their own initiative on Namibia, commencing with a *démarche* of the Five in Pretoria. This is why 16 March 1977 can be put on record as the date on which Namibia Contact Group (CG) was founded.[10]

In the context of those attempts at agreement, the Five lobbied at a meeting with leading UN representatives from Africa and the other non-aligned states on 17 March in favour of abandoning the previous course of fruitless confrontation and adopting a "new approach" to deal with the problems of Southern Africa. The "statement of principles" was to constitute the basis. As the Five's spokesman, Ivor Richard (Great Britain)

---

[10] DB 720 of 12.4.1977 from NY. Considering this varied and meandering course of events, it is surprising that, in Ambassador von Wechmar' recollection, the impetus behind the concept of the Namibia Initiative and founding of the CG had allegedly been the fruit of a creative duet of ideas between US Ambassador Young and himself performed within a week at the "beginning of 1977" (von Wechmar in "Die Vere-inten Nationen und deutsche VN-Politik – aus persönlicher Sicht", DGVN-Texte 39, UNO-Verlag Bonn 1991, pp.42/43). The fact that von Wechmar's memory had not precisely registered everything about this undertaking is evident from his astonishing assumption that SCR 385, adopted on 1 January 1976 and recognised by every expert in this field as the platform of the whole initiative, had not been passed until 1977 with his participation – and also his assertion that the "proximity talks" between those involved in the conflict had been an established CG practice whereas in fact only 2 "proximity talks" (1977 and 1979) are to be found among the over 20 negotiating arrangements which the CG had to undergo. This particular piece of misinforma-tion and essentially the whole version is repeated by von Wechmar in "Akteur in der Loge." Siedler-Verlag 2000, pp.313-315. Cf. also interviews, e.g. in Jabri pp.59 and 82. Young also seems to have perpetuated this legend in interviews, e.g., Engel/Sch-leicher p.272. Until then a local government politician in Atlanta, Young was first sent on a familiarisation trip around Africa by the State Department in January 1977. On 16 February, he had still said nothing to the other heads in New York about the idea of an Initiative by the Five on Namibia., although he did report that the Tanzanian President Nyerere had called for "dealing with Namibia" to be one of Washington's priorities (DB 293 of 17.2.1977 from NY).During the entire settlement process, the heads of the five UN Missions made hardly any major contributions to the concept, busying themselves rather with organisational arrangements and press conferences in New York. They were not present at most of the negotiations – in Cape Town/Preto-ria, Lusaka, Luanda, Gaborone, Maputo, Dar es Salaam, Lagos, Harare and Geneva. Even in New York, virtually all the internal CG strategy meetings, but also some important negotiations, took place without them.

added that the western SC members should form a "negotiating group" together with other UN members maintaining diplomatic relations with South Africa, with the mandate of entering into talks with Pretoria on Namibia. This did not herald an independent group of Five, nor was the idea of a *démarche* mentioned. The Africans stated that since they rejected any direct negotiation by a UN member with South Africa, they could not approve the assigning of a mandate to a "negotiating group" by the SC. The Libyan Ambassador added that the "negotiating group" could proceed on a voluntary basis. These statements strengthened the resolve of the Five not to let their later Namibia CG be constrained by a formal SC mandate to deliver constant official reporting to the SC, but to provide the SC with information at their own discretion.[11]

To the Five's relief, the SC debate was postponed *sine die* in April as events concerning Namibia appeared to be gaining in importance.[12] The proposal of a "negotiating group" was not pursued any further.

II "Proposals for stern action"

The Five found themselves under great time pressure in preparing the *démarche* in Pretoria.[13] They were aware that the South Africans were pushing rapidly ahead with their project for an "internal solution" (Namibia's "independence" at the end of 1978) and now wanted to create a *fait accompli* by having the Parliament in Cape Town adopt an interim constitution and the appointment of an interim government on 20 May 1977.[14]
The background to this project can be summarised as follows:
In September 1975, an assembly was convened at Pretoria's initiative in the *Turnhalle* in Windhoek with the task of drafting a constitution. The

---

[11] DB 488 of 17.3.1977 from NY.
[12] DB 680 of 4.4.1977 from NY.
[13] DB 481 of 16.3.1977 from NY and DB 609 of 28.3.1977 from NY.
[14] DB 741 of 14.4.1977 from NY.

large *Kaiserliche Deutsche Turnhalle* was part of a sports complex from the colonial era and had been converted into a conference facility. In line with the Odendaal Plan of 1962 and analogous to the system of Bantustanisation in South Africa, racial segregation of the so-called non-White population according to ethnic criteria and allocation of "homelands" to Blacks was far advanced in Namibia. According to this distribution, almost half the entire territory was to remain in the hands of Whites who then represented only about 11% of the population. Delegates from ten separate ethnic groups and delegates of the Whites had now been summoned to a "National Assembly" at the *Turnhalle*. In proceedings constantly controlled from Pretoria, this assembly delivered the desired draft of an interim constitution in 1977 which was intended to serve as the basis for an interim government.[15] The entire *Turnhalle* project was neither acceptable to the UN nor to the South West Africa People's Organization (SWAPO) nor to the CG. It was completely incompatible with SCR 385. Among other things, it was impossible to regard a "National Assembly" with 60 members as representative when the "Ovambos" (approx. 50% of the population, predominantly SWAPO supporters) had been allocated 12 seats, while smaller groups such as the "Rehoboth Basters" (approx. 2.5%) had 4 seats. In autumn 1977, Pretoria merged the eleven groups together into a party called the "Democratic Turnhalle Alliance" (DTA), in whose leadership the White Dirk Mudge always played the principal role.[16] For the CG *Turnhalle* remained the watchword for South Africa's manipulated attempt to found a "client state organized along racial and tribal lines" and avoid a fair UN regulation.[17] The "internal solution" remained South Africa's sometimes openly otherwise secretly pursued preference for a decade. The apartheid regime perceived every SCR 385 angle not only as the certain loss of its own sway over Namibia but above all as the beginning of a

---

[15] For details on this cf. Brenke, loc. cit. pp.20-22; Jabri loc. cit. pp.38-41.

[16] Brenke, loc. cit. p.22.

[17] Vance, loc. cit. p.273.

democratic contagion process and thus as a threat to White rule in South Africa itself. This fear was to prove realistic.

At the first meeting of the Namibia CG on 16 March 1977, the Americans had presented a draft text for the *démarche* to be conducted in Cape Town. Following consultations and several amendments, the draft was transmitted to capitals for approval on 28 March. The five Cape Town Ambassadors duly served the *démarche* on Prime Minister John Balthazar Vorster by delivering the text on 7 April. After a summary of SCR 385, section E read as follows:

> The Governments wish to make it clear that in the absence of early South African agreement to pursue a settlement which will meet the foregoing principles and be internationally acceptable, the Governments will be obliged to reconsider their previous positions regarding proposals for stern action by the United Nations and will be compelled to examine a new range of measures intended to obtain South African compliance with applicable resolutions of the United Nations Security Council concerning Namibia.

PM Vorster immediately understood the wording "stern action" as a serious signal and did not hesitate to declare his willingness to conduct talks with a CG delegation.

III "Not entirely successful"

When the CG met in New York on 12 April 1977 to plan preparation of the next step, the US representative referred to a State Department instruction which proposed conducting an advance exchange of ideas with South Africa's UN representative on the objectives of negotiations. Concurring with the other Four, the American UN representative also regarded this idea as virtually absurd. Premature revelation of the CG's current intentions might block all further courses of action.[18] Washington later accepted this standpoint.

---

[18] DB 720 of 12.4.1977 from NY.

The following day, Washington expressed misgivings about Cape Town as the location for the first CG encounter with South Africa. A more neutral venue, ideally New York, was preferable. The other Four disagreed, and even Don McHenry, Young's deputy, contradicted his headquarters. It was clear that the Five wanted something from South Africa. The opportunity to forestall the appointment of an interim government in Windhoek would be jeopardised if valuable time were now wasted negotiating the first venue. It took several days for the State Department to relent.[19]

The CG's objective had to be: to avoid the *Turnhalle* Interim Government and implement SCR 385, i.e. first and foremost, free elections under UN control for a constituent assembly, South Africa's withdrawal from Namibia, the release of political prisoners, permission for Namibians forced to live abroad for political reasons to return to the country and the abolition of racially discriminatory regulations.

Once the CG had drawn up its specific negotiating plan and the South African government had accepted 27 April as the date for talks to commence, the following persons were dispatched to Cape Town from New York: Don McHenry (USA), James Murray (Great Britain), Albert Thabault (France), Hans-Joachim Vergau (Germany) and Paul Lapointe (Canada).

In the years 1977 and 1978, this Quintet retained the lead role – closely coordinated with the respective foreign ministries – in the increasingly intensive preparatory work and virtually all major negotiations within the framework of the initiative. At the UN they were soon called "the Gang of Five". Together with this core Quintet, the five local Ambassadors (where available) always participated. In New York, the five heads of the UN missions also attended important events. Sometimes, for example during the initial rounds in Cape Town, leading officials from the capitals were in-

---

[19] For more on this interlude cf. DB 728 and 731 of 13.4.1977 both from NY and DB 752 of 15.4.1977 from NY.

volved.[20] In isolated cases, the Foreign Ministers put in a personal appearance.

The CG's internal rules of procedure were never set out in writing. Without a great deal of discussion, the arrangement right to the end was that there was no chairperson in New York but that the chair was assumed by whichever UN embassy hosted the meeting. The venue in New York initially rotated. Later, most meetings were held in the US and Canadian missions because of their proximity to the UN headquarters, and eventually almost all the meetings took place at the US mission. The role of spokesman vis-à-vis negotiating partners in Africa and the African media also rotated. The Five consistently prepared detailed "talking points" and wrote joint records for their capitals after each stage of negotiations.

On 27 April 1977, it was obvious in Cape Town that the unusual group visit from the capitals of South Africa's remaining major international partners was a sensation for all South African media. At the entrance to the government building, the CG was besieged by cameras and microphones.

PM Vorster received the five delegations in the Cabinet room immediately adjacent to his office. After an extremely friendly welcome, the PM stated quite emphatically that the problem concerned not only the SC and South Africa but above all "the people of South West Africa" and that representatives of the *Turnhalle* were available on the premises.

---

[20]   The Ambassadors of the Five in South Africa were: W.G. Bowdler (USA), Hans-Joachim Eick (Germany), J. Schricke (France), Sir D. Scott (Great Britain), G.K. Grande (Canada). On behalf of Germany the following Foreign Ministry officials joined the round: Walter Jesser (Africa Director), Helmut Müller (Head of the Southern Africa Desk). From 1977 to 1990, numerous members of the Foreign Service participated loyally and commendably in the German contribution to the overall diplomatic work of the CG, inter alia Karl Flittner, Wilhelm Haas, Uwe Hansen, Reinhard Hilger, Heinz-Norbert Holl, Leonhard Kremer, Wolfgang Massing, Hans-Ulrich Seidt, Cornelius Sommer, Ernst-Jörg von Studnitz, Christian Ueberschaer, Elisabeth Weiss. – Günter Wasserberg (Lusaka), Hans-Joachim Dunker (Luanda). Hans-Joachim Eick (1976-1980) and Ekkehard Eickhoff (1980-1982) rendered outstanding service as German Ambassadors in South Africa.

"I, for one, must in all sincerity impress upon you that you must not overlook these people. I strongly recommend you, talk to them". Without addressing this point, CG spokesman Don McHenry closed his reply with the following spontaneously chosen words:

> We are seeking an understanding in line with positive SCR proposals. For a long time all UN contacts with South Africa on Namibia have been bedevilled by controversy over certain legal issues. On those issues please let us from the outset agree to disagree - and set them aside.

Vorster acknowledged this with the hint of an approving smile.

The PM departed and FM Roelof F. Botha assumed the chair, assisted by his Under-Secretary, Brand Fourie and the Chief Legal Adviser, J.D. Viall.

It had not escaped the CG's notice that the *Turnhalle* delegation was already waiting in a side room. McHenry made it clear to Botha that contact with *Turnhalle* representatives at a later stage was not ruled out but that it was out of the question in parallel to the introductory talks. Botha showed his angry disappointment. After McHenry had presented the Five's objectives, Botha instantly singled out the demand that South Africa should suspend the appointment of the interim government. The PM was "irrevocably committed" to its immediate appointment. If the Five were firmly opposed, he saw no point in continuing the talks. After further CG persuasion, he continued by saying that he did not rule out the possibility of the PM initially not submitting the interim constitution to Parliament in Cape Town. However, the interim government was only an "administrative arrangement". In the interest of a central administration and because of the promises made, it was absolutely indispensable. Since the CG did not yield, the Foreign Ministers again threatened to abandon the talks but then scheduled an afternoon meeting following a British objection that there were still other important points to discuss.

CG spokesman Michael Shenstone (Canada) requested more specific details on the "administrative arrangement". Botha's long-winded description reinforced the CG's suspicion that it was merely the *Turnhalle* concept under a different guise. The CG asked for even more precise information at a later meeting.

On the subject of UN supervision of the elections, Botha referred to the *Turnhalle's* firm conviction that the UN were biased, as demonstrated by the aggressive tone of GA Resolutions, especially the designation of SWAPO as "sole and authentic representative". The CG insisted that the SC had never pursued this line. The CG pointed now – and at the following meeting – to past experience which guaranteed that the Secretary-General (SG) would ensure a fair UN role with carefully selected UNTAG personnel, thus displaying a great deal of understanding even at this early stage for South Africa's problem with UN "impartiality", which would have to be addressed more directly at a much later date.[21]

When Botha explained on the morning of 28 April that Parliament would give the PM unconditional free rein to appoint the interim government by decree, but in turn would not guarantee a clear rejection of the ethnically based concept, Murray virtually implored him to reconsider, saying that South Africa should understand that this was not a legal but a political problem and that South Africa was pulling the rug out from under the CG in New York by establishing *faits accomplis*.

During the afternoon session, PM Vorster confirmed the decision to suspend enactment of the *Turnhalle* constitution for the time being, but insisted on the appointment of a "Central Administrative Authority" (CAA) until the elections. The intention was to establish a Council of Ministers modelled on the interim government (chairperson and 11 ministers, retaining the ethnic distribution), "virtually a self-administering body". Asked about the timing, the PM replied, uttering the first words probably by mistake: "If you give me green light I can establish it in a couple of weeks." This was no help to the CG. When Murray suggested that South Africa

---

21 For more on "impartiality" cf Annex D.

could simply appoint a South African "Resident Administrator", Vorster asked with pathos where "short of the Archangel Gabriel" he was supposed to find a suitably qualified man and whether he would not then be accused of appointing a dictator. The CG made it clear that it needed more information from South Africa on the design of the problematical CAA.

Vorster was flexible in principle on the role of the UN, but ruled out "control" as unacceptable. "The control formula would make my position impossible. I cannot sell this to my people." The wording should be "UN involvement".

Political prisoners could be released as long as they had not been convicted of a criminal offence. Namibians in exile could return if they came back peacefully and unarmed. Discriminatory provisions, if any such existed, would be abolished within the framework of electoral regulations.

The two meetings which concluded this round began on 29 April, with Ambassador Hans-Joachim Eick (Germany) as CG spokesman. He presented the CG draft of a joint record which gave rise to a rather abstract debate about the future economic responsibility for Namibia. Vorster then took exception to the competencies envisaged for the UN Special Representative (UNSR). Submitting the regulations for electoral proceedings for him "to approve" or subjecting the elections themselves to his "supervision and control" was out of the question. Equally, "to oversee" or "to monitor" went too far. After a long tug-of-war, the CG reluctantly accepted the following compromise wording which verges on the comical:

> "He would have to be satisfied as to the fairness of the regulations ..." and
> "he would have to satisfy himself, at all stages, as to the fairness of the campaign process as well as the election itself."

The Five felt distinctly uncomfortable with this concession since it meant deviating from the wording of SCR 385. They left no one in any doubt that they would have to interpret this formulation in New York as "supervision and control".

While McHenry called the discussions "frank and useful" and the first round "not entirely successful" in his concluding remarks, Vorster expressed his gratitude for the spirit of accommodation. "I frankly think that we can all learn a lesson from this meeting and in the future refer to it. We achieved a great lot and I sincerely hope you will be able to sell it."[22]

The CG had not neglected to announce its next steps openly to the South Africans, namely immediate contact with everyone they considered it appropriate to inform. This was primarily SG Kurt Waldheim, SWAPO, the future UN Special Representative Maarti Ahtisaari (Finnish), the Council for Namibia, the chair of the UN Anti-Apartheid-Committee, the Front-Line States (FLS) and Nigeria, as well as the *Turnhalle* in Windhoek and other interested forces (e.g. the small Federal Party, opposed to the *Turnhalle* and led by a White, and representatives of the Churches). The CG thus adhered to its principle of coherent transparency as a compelling prerequisite for confidence building, a principle it never abandoned. In particular, the CG was constantly aware that it depended on the SC for support and, at least for the adoption of the UNTAG budget, also on the GA. From the African side, especially the FLS and Nigeria which was always included as the strongest force within the African group at the time, it urgently required support in dealing with SWAPO.

All these briefings took place between 1 and 15 May 1977. Reactions were guarded and on the African side sceptical, in some quarters suspicious and disapproving of the CG's contacts with the *Turnhalle*. However, general opposition to the Five's Initiative was not expressed in any of the talks.

One partner body which remained particularly critical was the UN Council for Namibia. It consisted of 11 members, almost all of whom came from the non-aligned states, predominantly from Africa. After South Africa's mandate was revoked in 1966, the GA established the Council for Namibia in 1967 to administer Namibia and prepare it for independ-

---

22 Course of the first round in Cape Town: DB 76 and DB 77 of 27.4.1977, DB 80 and 81 of 28.4.1977, DB to Section 312 of 29.4.1977 – all from Cape Town.

ence. But as South Africa would not budge and refused to recognise the Council, the latter remained in New York nursing its frustration, roundly condemned South Africa and its business partners and regarded the CG initiative as trespassing on its territory. The CG kept the Council for Namibia informed but otherwise managed to hold it at bay.[23]

On 26 May, the CG was greatly disillusioned by McHenry's report on a recent meeting in Vienna between US Vice-President Mondale and PM Vorster. Regardless of the assurances he had given the CG, Vorster indicated his intention *inter alia* to impose the entire *Turnhalle* concept *de facto* on Namibia. The commencement of South African withdrawal could only be considered after independence. At the same time, he appeared in a curious hurry to convene a second CG round in Cape Town. Vance accurately drew the following conclusion:

> ... the South Africans intended to follow a two-track strategy: preparing the option of an internal settlement, while at the same time continuing to explore the possibilities for a wider solution.[24]

It was obvious to the Five that considerably more detailed clarifications and concessions from SA were a prerequisite for any further mediation in the Namibia conflict. They had to return to Cape Town.

IV The lights go out in the *Turnhalle*

A renewed *démarche* by the Ambassadors in South Africa on 30 May 1977 secured Vorster's approval to conduct further talks with the CG in Cape Town

---

[23]   For more on the CG's confidence-building transparency work: DB 92 of 3.5.1977 from Windhoek as well as DB 937, DB 938 and DB 941 of 5.5.1977, DB 948 of 6.5.1977, DB 957 of 6.5.1977, DB 978 of 10.5.1977, DB 982 of 10.5.1977, DB 999 of 11.5.1977 – all from NY – foundation of the Council for Namibia: GA/Res 2248 (S-V) of 19.5.1967; cf. also Brenke, loc. cit. p.15; dissolution of the Council for Namibia A/Res/44/243 of 11.9.1990.

[24]   Vance, loc. cit. p.278; cf. also DB 1139 of 26.5.1977 from NY.

on 8-10 June. The CG's prime objectives were to achieve a regulation in line with SCR 385 on issues concerning the transitional administration (CAA), shaping the UN role and South Africa's gradual withdrawal.[25]

At the discussions on the morning of 8 June, which were once again opened by PM Vorster but then chaired by FM Botha in the presence of Under-Secretary Fourie and legal adviser Viall, the Five[26] had to resist Botha's stubborn attempts to adhere to a purely Namibian CAA, with the ethnically divided *Turnhalle* parliamentarians playing a decisive role, and fend off solutions which guaranteed SA clear administrative responsibility during the transitional process. It became clear that the determining factor was not so much promises made to the *Turnhalle* but to an even greater extent concerns that measures incompatible with apartheid, e.g. the abolition of racially discriminatory regulations in Namibia, might undermine the stability of the system in South Africa itself, the more openly South African authority was assumed in Windhoek.

At the same time, the South African side had claimed that Walvis Bay belonged to the Cape Province, prompting a strong recommendation from the CG not to prejudge this issue with any further acts of state but to keep it open for later negotiation.

In the afternoon, Vorster himself seemed highly agitated, bizarrely claiming that the *Turnhalle* had done more for a peaceful settlement than the Five, the UN and South Africa together; that only they could safeguard territorial unity. "You are shooting down *Turnhalle* thus allowing me to pull out of South West Africa straight away regardless of the consequences or to go ahead with *Turnhalle* regardless of the international reaction!" He constantly implied that the CG risked aborting the round.

Shortly before the meeting was suspended, FM Botha was summoned to the telephone in an adjacent room. When the phone call dragged on,

---

[25]   DB 1197 of 2.6.1977 from NY.

[26]   Ambassadors of the Five participating together with the Quintet as in footnote 20.

the PM followed him. The Five were left behind, tensely waiting. Then Botha returned alone and declaimed with great dramatic effect:

The situation had come to a head. The *Turnhalle* delegates categorically rejected any form of CAA that did not include the 11 ethnic representatives of the *Turnhalle* and that exceeded a membership of 17.

While the Five were still full of dismay, he proclaimed that there was yet another development: The PM thought it possible to be released from his "commitment" and to appoint just a single South African Administrator-General instead of the CAA. More on that was to follow the next day.

That was indeed what Vorster announced on 9 June, explaining that the Administrator-General (AG), whom he intended to appoint as early as August, would have to act impartially; no political advisory body was envisaged. In the meantime, the UNSR and his team should also be on hand. Elections were to be held by the end of December 1977, as the Namibians could no longer be subjected to "a political vacuum", the state of political suspense now provoked by the CG.

The CG counselled greater realism with regard to timing. It now had to tackle the difficult task of generating support for the concept and its new elements at the UN and, above all, in the SC. Under no circumstances would the SG commence UNTAG preparations without a prior SC mandate.

Considerable agreement on shaping the UN role was achieved during this round, whilst little specific progress was made on the crucial issue of South Africa's withdrawal. Nor could other demands under SCR 385 be finally settled. On 10 June, a confidential record was negotiated in tough clashes with Vorster. One of the results recorded was that, within the framework of the transition process, all racially discriminatory regulations should be abolished by the AG (in other words, by the South Africans themselves). South Africa insisted on making the release of political prisoners from Namibia in the FLS a condition for the release of its own prisoners, whilst the CG maintained the position that political prisoners everywhere should be released. It would uphold this position everywhere and could not accept

> ... that the release of such persons in one country should be contingent on the release of persons elsewhere.[27]

When the round concluded, the CG realised that encouraging progress had been made with complete exclusion of the *Turnhalle*, but that there were still high hurdles to be overcome. As it had done after the first round, the CG once again informed all major interested parties, tailoring the content to the respective recipients and involving virtually the whole of Africa. Out of loyalty to SWAPO's concerns, African reactions remained predominantly sceptical but without adopting a confrontational position on the CG's efforts.

SG Waldheim, who invariably sought the backing of a secure UN majority, continued referring for weeks to the conventional decision-making process in the SC and GA (competency of the Council for Namibia / South Africa's presence in Namibia, and thus also a South African Administrator-General, illegal), persisting in his objection that results achieved so far did not constitute an adequate basis for what he considered an indispensable, specific SC mandate to prepare UNTAG. He rejected the CG's idea of initially taking SCR 385 as a basis and independent of the Council for Namibia, appointing a trusted member of his staff *ad personam* as UNSR.[28] The CG was left with the impression that it had to push the UN

---

[27] Course of the second round in Cape Town: DB of 7.6.1977 (delegation report no. 1 to Section 312); DB 108 of 8.6.1977; DB 109 of 8.6.1977; DB 111 of 9.6.1977; DB 113 of 9.6.1977; DB 114 of 10.6.1977; DB 115 of 11.6.1977 – all from Cape Town.

[28] DB 1339 of 17.6.1977 from NY; DB 1581 of 13.7.1977 from NY; DB 1622 of 21.7.1977 from NY.

process ahead with its own proposals on UNTAG. It was now also crucial to bring SWAPO round to the idea of initial, intensive consultations.[29]

Because the Africans had protested so vehemently the last time, there was no official briefing in Windhoek. The leading White *Turnhalle* representative, Dirk Mudge, was informed in New York, and he took the occasion to outline a future role for the *Turnhalle* parties in the election campaign as an alliance under his leadership (DTA). Underlying Mudge's words was the speculation that SWAPO and the Africa Group would in any case thwart the CG's plans, an idea which was obviously central to all South Africa's concessions.[30] A letter from SWAPO President Sam Nujoma might have put a damper on all this. In response to his briefing in Lusaka on 22 June, he wrote to the UN mission of the USA:

Concerning the current talks of the Contact Group of the western five members of the Security Council with South Africa regarding Namibia and their efforts to keep SWAPO informed about finding a basis for a negotiated settlement of the Namibian problem, SWAPO wishes to state the following:

1. These talks must always be within the framework of the UN for the sole purpose of the full implementation of all outstanding resolutions and decisions of the UN on Namibia, especially SCR 385 (1976).

2. In this context, SWAPO appreciates the efforts of the Contact Group and urges all other states, members of the UN, to facilitate individually and collectively the success of this undertaking.

3. SWAPO would, however, like to advise strongly that, in so far as contacting or briefing SWAPO whether internal or external by the Contact Group is concerned, this must now be centralised and restricted to our Permanent Observer Mission to the UN in New York. In this connection, SWAPO has designated comrade Theo-Ben Gurirab, who is a member of the National Executive Committee and also our Permanent Observer Representative there. Henceforth all dealings of the Contact Group with SWAPO must be only through him.

---

[29]   DB 1390 of 22.6.1977 from NY.
[30]   DB 1284 of 13.6.1977 from NY; DB 1383 of 22.6.1977 from NY.

In conclusion, accept, Sir, the assurances of our highest consideration.

Sincerely yours

Sam Nujoma[31]

V From SWAPO's point of view all power belongs to the United Nations

SWAPO had long upheld its position, confirmed by the GA in 1976 in contradiction with SCR 385, that it was the "sole and authentic representative of the Namibian people" and could demand the "immediate transfer of power" – if not to SWAPO itself, then at least to the UN.[32] The CG had only ever dealt with this one liberation movement.

Sam Nujoma arrived in New York on 6 August 1977 together with 9 SWAPO delegates, among them Gurirab and other members of the "Executive Committee". Negotiations with the CG were held at the Ralph Bunche Institute, located on the corner of Fifth Avenue and 42nd Street, on 8-11 August. The CG had preferred this more neutral location to a meeting room where UN business was normally conducted or one of their UN missions.

The following is an extract from Nujoma's introductory statement of 8 August:

> ... It is our considered opinion, however, that to date nothing substantial has been achieved which would warrant optimism on our part. If anything, the developments thus far have confirmed our grave doubts about South Africa's sincerity and readiness to end her occupation of Namibia.

---

[31]   DB 1420 of 27.6.1977 from NY.

[32]   The GA had already confirmed SWAPO as the "authentic representative" in Resolution 28/3111 of 12.12.1973. In line with the OAU, SWAPO was then accorded the predicate "sole and authentic" at the 31st GA. on 20.12.1976 in Res. 31/146 and granted observer status in Res. 152. For more on Germany's evaluation of SWAPO at the time, cf. DB 2188 of 24.9 and DB 3426 of 3.12.1976, both from NY.

... The agreement concerning the so-called Administrator-General has nothing to do with SCR 385; and the very fact that South Africa has gone ahead with the appointment of the so-called Administrator-General without reference to the UN is a clear indication that the whole exercise is being deliberately conducted outside the framework of SCR 385. Furthermore, the calculated coining of a new concept of UN "involvement" as opposed to <u>UN supervision and control</u> is another clear indication that there is an attempt to evade UN's full and explicit role in the solution of the conflict.

... South Africa must publicly announce in categorical terms that it will fully respect and observe the territorial integrity of Namibia.

... South Africa must undertake publicly to withdraw all her armed forces from Namibia as a precondition to the holding of elections. South Africa must unreservedly accept the principle of free elections in Namibia based on universal adult suffrage.

... Upon South Africa publicly committing herself to the principles above, talks will then be held between SWAPO, UN and South Africa on the mechanics and modalities involved in the achievement of independence.

After South Africa has publicly undertaken to withdraw all her forces from Namibia, a logistical program for such withdrawal will be discussed. SWAPO appreciates the fact that such withdrawal can reasonably not take place over night and, that in order to create a climate of peace leading to peaceful transition,

... such withdrawal should be inter-changeably phased-out, that is, the UN peace-keeping force taking over the positions of the withdrawing South African armed forces. This process should start immediately and should not take more than three months from the date of agreement on the withdrawal of all South Africa armed forces. During this withdrawal period, the UN moves its administrative machinery into the country to take over the administration and public security and embarks on the organization for elections.

SWAPO commits itself to fair, genuine and democratic elections under UN <u>supervision</u> and <u>control</u>.

... such elections should take place after the conditions on withdrawal of the armed forces as stipulated above have been fulfilled ...

In discussions on 9 August, Nujoma remained adamant on all these positions, in particular that South African rule had to be replaced swiftly by unrestricted UN rule. The functions and powers of the UNSR had to be set out in black and white and he had to have a "veto right" vis-à-vis the AG. On the latter point, the CG managed to explain that it was also its understanding that the AG would not be able to act without the UNSR's consent. Overall, the CG advised realistic moderation: irrespective of UN dogmatism, it was now also in SWAPO's interests to persuade South Africa to accept an agreed settlement, i.e. to yield voluntarily. On a positive note, acceptance of democratic elections meant that the presumptuous claim to sole representation had been dropped.

On 10 and 11 August, acceptance of an AG was achieved – always acting with UNSR approval. This was a strenuous process, especially as Vorster had ignored the CG's advice to co-ordinate the announcement of an AG with the appointment of the UNSR and had publicly proclaimed the South African Marthinus Steyn (a judge) as AG on 6 July 1977. He was formally appointed with effect from 1 September.

SWAPO offered a cease-fire, following which the remaining South African troops were to be assembled at a UN-supervised base. Such "confinement to bases" could also be considered for SWAPO fighters inside Namibia. The question of how to control SWAPO units in Angola and Zambia remained unresolved. In any case, all South African military had to have left Namibia before the election campaign began. The police, who could retain their role under supervision, as well as para-military security forces were to be disarmed. As far as the UN presence was concerned, deploying non-combatant military "observers" was insufficient; a 5,000-strong, powerful "peace-keeping force" had to be brought in. SWAPO would not now ask the SC to prepare UNTAG. An SC mandate was essential prior to every actual UN operation in Namibia. But SWAPO had no objection to the SG starting advanced planning now on the basis of SCR 385.[33]

In the light of this result, SG Waldheim was prepared to commence the advance planning for UNTAG without a further SC mandate.[34]

On 19 August 1977, the five Ambassadors in Pretoria notified the South African government of this outcome in their third *démarche*. They emphasised that it was now an urgent priority for South Africa to present a concrete plan for the phased withdrawal of its armed forces. The FLS and Nigeria were also fully briefed in their respective capitals.[35]

VI Pretoria juggling with its troop numbers

Following a fourth *démarche* on 12 September, a third round was agreed with South Africa in Pretoria scheduled to begin on 22 September.[36]

PM Vorster opened the talks with the surprising claim – untenable in the light of the two preceding rounds – that there had been no previous talk of a South African troop withdrawal. This was "totally unacceptable!" before a new government had been installed in an independent Namibia. By contrast, FM Botha submitted a written proposal at the meetings he chaired on 23 September: a gradual withdrawal of South African troops relative to the reduction in the threat posed by SWAPO and other forces operating from Angola. The following explanation was given:

---

[33] Course of the first SWAPO round: DB 1757 of 8.8.1977; DB 1770 of 9.8.1977; DB 1776 of 10.8.1977; DB 1790 of 11.8.1977; DB 1801 of 12.8.1977 - all from NY.

[34] DB 1871 of 23.8.1977 from NY.

[35] DB 1835 of 17.8.1977 from NY; DB 1841 of 18.8.1977 from NY; DB 1910 of 29.8.1977 from NY.

[36] Ambassadors of the Five participating together with the Quintet as in footnote 20. Africa Director in Bonn from September 1977 to September 1979, active and always full of ideas, was Helmut Müller (his successor until 1984 was Wilhelm Haas); Müller took part in this South Africa round and in several of the later negotiations.

The presence of substantial Cuban forces on the Angolan side. ... With the present South African forces in South West Africa, we are satisfied that no Cuban move against the territory would take place. However, as long as the Cubans are there, it would be irresponsible not to provide for possible incursions.[37]

The Cubans had to vacate the area south of the Benguela railway line.

There were also considerable SWAPO forces in Angola dangerously close to the border. They had to be deployed back behind a border north of Mocamedes-Serpa-Pinto and kept under surveillance there. All violent SWAPO activities in Namibia had to be suspended. Under these preconditions, South African troops (20,000 men) could be kept concentrated in their current bases, possibly under the supervision of "UN observers". These troops could be gradually reduced to 8,000, which had to remain in the country until after the elections to be held on 31 January 1978. If the Cubans were withdrawn, this number could be reduced still further.

In order to secure a continuation of the round, the delegates of the Five assigned their core Quintet the task of conducting mediating talks with FM Botha and Under-Secretary Fourie in the latter's flat that evening. Botha gave an assurance that the para-military units would also be dissolved as part of the gradual reduction ("commandos will be demobbed" and the AG would have the Bantustan "regional security forces" at his disposal in agreement with the UNSR). The figure of 8,000 referred only to regular troops. Real UN military units were not acceptable, and the number of UN personnel had to remain limited ("not into the thousands"). Only a "UN military observer team" under the supervision of the UNSR was conceivable as monitors. The CG warned of unrealistic plans with regard to figures and the election date.

Before the meeting on 24 September, the Five had discovered that South Africa only had a total of 8,000 regular troops deployed in Namibia.

---

[37]   DB 391 of 25.9.1977 from Pretoria.

They confronted Botha during the meeting with the accusation that the reduction was therefore largely restricted to reservists and para-military commandos who could be re-activated within 2 hours. Although visibly annoyed, Botha relented and promised further clarification. He also appeared no longer interested in adhering to the utopian demand for Cuban withdrawal, asking merely for understanding with regard to alleged concerns about Namibia's security. The South Africans never again raised the Cuban presence during the entire CG negotiating process.

Prompted by public statements from PM Vorster, the CG once again expressed its reservations about South Africa's position on the status of Walvis Bay.

The Five presented a timetable for all necessary UN and South African steps, providing for elections to a constituent assembly on 1 July and independence in December 1978. Apart from agreeing to the SG's proposal to appoint Martti Ahtisaari as UNSR, Botha's reaction was dismissive. In view of all these unreasonable demands, South Africa was no longer interested in an international settlement. It was boldly asserted in public that sanctions could not force South Africa to capitulate.

The CG was under no illusion about the looming crisis. Should Pretoria now indeed assume that sanctions were bearable and international isolation inevitable, South Africa's two main motives for constructive engagement with the CG initiative would disappear. In fact, the South Africans were by no means so composed about the spectre of Chapter VII. But behind their calculations was the belief that in the West, above all in the USA and the Federal Republic of Germany, there was a powerful, silent majority of sympathisers who could be addressed directly over the heads of their misguided governments and persuaded to adopt a more tolerant approach to the *apartheid* system. The Five left no stone unturned in their efforts to convince Botha of the catastrophic consequences that a failure of the initiative would have in the UN.

On Monday, 26 September 1977, Botha came up with new proposals. On the topic of withdrawal, South Africa now intended to reduce its "active" troops to 1,400 (concentrated at the northern base of Oshivelo) by February 1978. However, a further 2,600 soldiers had to remain as "auxiliary personnel" (supplies, supervision of the many other military bases, etc.). South Africa had to take into account the forces deployed close to the border in Southern Angola. Should the Five continue to reject the proposal of redeploying them further north, South Africa at least required assurances about the way in which these troops would be supervised. If armed SWAPO units were allowed to move around freely in the area, cross-border aggression had to be expected at any time. Botha now named the end of March 1978 as the latest possible election date.

During the concluding session chaired by PM Vorster on the afternoon of 26 September, these proposals were not set out as a formal ultimatum, but the PM gave the CG no sign of any prospects of further concessions.[38]

At a meeting with representatives from Angola, Zambia, Botswana, Tanzania, Mozambique and Nigeria in New York on 5 October, the CG managed to give the Africans the impression that further negotiations were still meaningful, despite all the inadequacies of the new state of affairs, and that a fresh encounter with SWAPO was justified.[39]

SG Waldheim was informed on 7 October and the Council for Namibia on 11 October.

A second round with SWAPO at the German UN mission in New York (then located at 600 Third Avenue) was scheduled to begin on 14 October. Surprisingly, Nujoma rejected this venue at the last moment, stating that SWAPO would not set foot in the Mission of a State which

---

[38]   Course of the third round with South Africa: DB 387 of 23.9.1977; DB 391 of 25.9.1977; DB 392 of 25.9.1977; DB 393 of 25.9.1977; DB 396 of 26.9.1977 – all from Pretoria.

[39]   DB 2354 of 6.10.1977 from New York.

maintained a Consulate in Windhoek.[40] The round was relocated to the British UN mission. The SWAPO delegation consisted of President Sam Nujoma, Hidipo Hamutenya, Theo-Ben Gurirab, Aaron Shihepo, Ngarikutuke Tjiriange and Bomani. On the CG side, the core Quintet led the negotiations, supported by Africa experts from the respective capitals. Murray (Great Britain) brought with him a young and extremely bright assistant from the British UN Mission, Tom Richardson, who made a major contribution in 1977/78, above all to written CG documents. In addition to the established member Paul Lapointe, the Canadian UN Mission sent Verona Edelstein who long remained a constructive and helpful colleague. The heads of the five UN missions were also present from time to time.

After a briefing on the third round in Pretoria, the meeting was adjourned.

On 15 October, Nujoma reiterated SWAPO's willingness to accept a formal ceasefire. All South African troops had to leave Namibia before preparations for the election campaign began, if possible by 31 January 1978, with UN peacekeepers deploying at the same time. The presence of residual South African troops was unacceptable since they had such an intimidating effect on the population after so many years of terrorist oppression that fair elections for all would be impossible. SWAPO fighters should be drawn together at bases within Namibia and placed under UN supervision. In so far as the administration was involved in organising the elections, everything had to be conducted in accordance with the UNSR, whose duty was also to supervise all the rest of the administration. The AG's role was to consist solely of "answering questions". The political process was to be conducted over a 9-month period beginning in December 1977, concluding with independence in August 1978.

---

[40] The Consulate of the Federal Republic of Germany inevitably had to be accredited with the South African government and was therefore incompatible with the virtually unanimous position adopted in the UN that SA's presence in Namibia was illegal. Cf. SCR 276 (1970); confirmed by the ICJ Advisory Opinion of 1971.

SWAPO rejected elections to a constituent assembly. For them it was exclusively a matter of electing the party that would form the new government. Its party programme would then represent the new constitution.

No major SWAPO concessions could be obtained at further meetings on 17 and 19 October. But by showing that it was honestly interested in listening and by exposing South Africa's hard-line positions, the CG was nevertheless able to bolster confidence in its role as impartial mediator and generate understanding for the extent of its difficulties. The impression also remained that the last word had yet not been spoken on South Africa's early and complete withdrawal. In later confidential talks, Hamutenya indicated to the German Quintet member that SWAPO could accept a small residual South African contingent under UN supervision if it were confined to a base that was not in the northern border area like Oshivelo but "perhaps in Grootfontein".[41]

The Five had already decided on 13 October to conduct a fifth *démarche* in Pretoria to coincide with the SWAPO round so as not to appear as a consequence of it. The *démarche* was duly made to FM Botha on 17 October. The South Africans were informed in no uncertain terms that their previous positions on the numbers and the stationing and supply of the remaining South African military forces (4,000 in total) were unacceptable. Clear assurances were also required that "commandos" and "citizen forces" based in Namibia but placed at South Africa's military disposal, plus about 1,600 "regional forces", would be effectively disarmed. This had to be done under UN control, for which UN military personnel was indispensable. Furthermore, South Africa was warned not to announce an early election date on its own authority. After a general rebuff from Botha, the Five received a written South African statement on 21 October, setting out in even greater detail why it was supposedly essential for the 4,000 troops to

---

[41] Course of the second SWAPO round: DB 2447 of 12.10.1977; DB 2491 of 14.10.1977; DB 2497 of 15.10.1977; DB 2514 of 17.10.1977; DB 2590 of 20.10.1977 – all from NY.

remain. However, the statement concluded by describing the threat posed by the military forces in Angola close to the border as the main motive for the high number. "If the threat were shown to be minor, one could argue that South African forces could be reduced still further."[42]

In response, the five Ambassadors served a sixth *démarche* on Under-Secretary Fourie in Pretoria on 21 November 1977. The CG now signalled its determination to draft a compromise package itself, by evaluating the positions which South Africa and SWAPO would eventually bring themselves to accept. However, these positions were still too far apart. South Africa had to understand why the international community did not regard the general military constellation in Angola as justification for large numbers of South African troops to remain in Namibia. As far as the SWAPO units in Angola were concerned, the CG wanted to reach an agreement with Angola on appropriate controls. The CG also understood SA's concerns about security within Namibia and was prepared to urge the FLS and SWAPO to accept a limited South African contingent. But this extremely difficult project was doomed to failure if South Africa did not considerably reduce its troop numbers and their collection points and accept appropriate numbers of UN military personnel.

Under-Secretary Fourie remained remarkably civil and sought to convey the impression of a willingness to reach an understanding, but did not offer the slightest hope of any such concessions from Pretoria.[43]

VII The Security Council sends Pretoria a warning signal

The CG was not expecting a good atmosphere. The Security Council had just taught Pretoria a bitter lesson. On 4 November 1977, a man-

---

[42]   *Démarches* in Pretoria on 17 and 21 October 1977: DB 2468 of 13.10.1977; DB 2494 of 14.10.1977; DB 2496 of 15.10.1977 – all from NY; DB 448 of 21.10.1977 from Pretoria.

[43]   DB 2977 of 10.11.1977 from NY; DB 518 of 22.11.1977 from Pretoria.

datory arms embargo had been unanimously imposed on South Africa, a result of the resumed South Africa debate postponed in April. This application of Chapter VII of the Charter was an event of historic significance in UN politics. Only once before had the SC ordered binding compulsory measures, namely economic sanctions on Rhodesia in 1966. Now the SC did not target Namibia directly but made a frontal attack on the apartheid system in South Africa itself with the opening words of the Preamble to SCR 418:

> ... Strongly condemning the South African Government for its resort to massive violence against and killings of the African people, including school children and students and others opposing racial discrimination, and calling upon that Government urgently to end violence against the African people and to take urgent steps to eliminate apartheid and racial discrimination.

In 1977, however, and for a further 20 years, the SC was dominated by an inhibition about assessing human rights violations within a State as a threat to international peace and thus no longer treating it as an "internal affair", which was outside the SC's purview under Article 2, paragraph 7 of the Charter.[44] Moreover, the GA (and not the SC) was the main UN forum at which, after over two decades of debates, international public opinion gradually began to assert itself despite Article 2: massive human rights violations, even if they only occurred within a State, concerned everyone and impinged on collective security. And it was precisely opposition to apartheid, for many years a central item on the GA's AGda, which lent considerable impetus to this development.

---

[44]   It emerges from an instruction issued by Redies (Section 230) on 19.3.1977 that, during those weeks, the French FM de Guiringaud had still advanced the view in a letter to FM Vance that, since *apartheid* was an internal affair of a sovereign State, he did not consider it admissible to go beyond an appeal to South Africa and to point out to South Africa how it should establish equal rights in its own country. For more on the principle of non-intervention cf. Kunig, loc. cit. pp.374-380 and pp.391-401; on SCR 418 (1977) cf. Franck, Fairness pp.224-231.

In 1977, the SC supplemented its denouncement of apartheid with a charge of violating international peace in the classical sense. Paragraphs 2 and 7 of the Preamble to SCR 418 read as follows:

> Recognizing that the military build-up by South Africa and its persistent acts of aggression against the neighbouring States seriously disturb the security of those States.

> Considering that the policies and acts of the South African Government are fraught with danger to international peace and security ...

Those SC Members guilty or suspected of having permitted arms supplies to South Africa – namely the USA, Great Britain, France and the Federal Republic of Germany – wanted to divert attention from the critical finger-pointing in their direction and, in a strange reverse formula, succeeded in portraying the acquisition rather than the supply of arms as the threat to peace:

> Determines, having regard to the policies and acts of the South African Government, that the acquisition by South Africa of arms and related material constitutes a threat to the maintenance of international peace and security.

The embargo itself did not have a radical effect on Pretoria since South Africa already possessed a largely autonomous arms production capability. But this UN sanction forced Pretoria to recognise that the Five no longer guaranteed absolute protection against Chapter VII. This change shattered the already shaky confidence of the South African leadership that the West was predominantly interested in the continued stability of its system. Were they perhaps not safe from comprehensive UN economic sanctions after all? In talks with the CG Quintet about details of the settlement plan in New York on 7 November, Under-Secretary Brand Fourie suppressed his anger at western unpredictability; on the contrary, he was remarkably co-operative.[45]

---

[45]   DB 2887 of 7.11.1977 from NY.

On 31 October 1977, Germany finally closed its Consulate in Windhoek and was thus able to enhance the credibility of the German CG role in the eyes of the Africans.

VIII Travelling diplomacy with the Five's proposal

The CG had played all its cards in the bilateral dialogue with South Africa and SWAPO. As mediators, it was now up to the Five to present their own settlement proposal. The main points of the proposal finalised on 4 November 1977 were:

– In accordance with SCR 385, free and fair elections under UN supervision and control for a constituent assembly.

– Prior to the elections, the release of all political prisoners detained by South Africa.

– Permission for all Namibians living outside the country to return freely and peacefully prior to the elections. UN control to ensure that Namibians who do not return are staying away voluntarily.

– Repeal of all discriminatory or otherwise restrictive regulations inhibiting free participation in the political process by the AG in agreement with the UNSR.

– Ceasefire with the following provisions:

(a) A cessation of all hostilities and the restriction of all SA and SWAPO armed forces to existing bases under UN supervision;

(b) Prior to the beginning of the election campaign, a phased withdrawal of all but 1,500 South African troops who would be restricted to a base under UN supervision and withdrawn after the elections.

(c) Demobilisation of the "citizen forces, commandos and ethnic forces" and dismantling of their command structures;

(d) Deployment of a UNTAG military component of about 2,000 men, with the maximum number to be determined by operational and logistical requirements;

(e) Peaceful return of Namibians through designated entry points, to participate freely in the political process;

(f) Closure of all SWAPO bases when the elections have been concluded.

– In agreement with the UNSR, the AG will maintain law and order with the help of the remaining police, removing unsuitable personnel in advance. The UNSR will guarantee that there is no intimidation or interference in the political process.

– After the elections, adoption of a Constitution by the Constituent Assembly and installation of a government before the end of 1978.[46]

The CG was aware that item (a) of the ceasefire arrangement also included the problem of UN control of SWAPO bases in Zambia and Angola.

The Five did not want to take this settlement proposal immediately to the conflicting parties but to submit it first to the FLS and Nigeria in agreement with the SG. A final version was not to be drafted until after careful discussion with them. The core Quintet was consequently dispatched to Dar es Salaam (Tanzania), Maputo (Mozambique), Gaborone (Botswana), Lusaka (Zambia), Luanda (Angola) and Lagos (Nigeria) for consultations.

On 21 November, President Julius Nyerere and FM Benjamin Mkapa received the CG with clear signs of a willingness to reach an understanding. He indicated that 1,500 remaining South African troops were tolerable in his view but that if he were speaking on behalf of SWAPO, he would then demand twice the number of UN personnel. This was the level necessary to counter SWAPO's understandable basic position (no remaining South African troops). When Murray (Great Britain) pointed out the cost of such

---

[46] DB 2854 of 4.11.1977 from NY.

high numbers of UN personnel, Nyerere countered that no one would be happier to see the venture fail than Pretoria and Moscow. The Soviet Union in particular would prefer no settlement; it regarded continued conflict as an advantage, especially as SWAPO might not be sufficiently Marxist in its eyes to guarantee a regime in Namibia that would serve its interests. South Africa's desire for early elections was to be refused. SWAPO would win the elections but was entitled to sufficient time "to appear before the people". If SWAPO lost the elections, there would be no chance for peace. Nyerere referred with concern to the danger of a negative impact which failure of the Namibia Initiative would have on efforts to reach a settlement for Rhodesia. He encouraged the CG to contact Angola. President Agostino Neto wanted peace in the South, which required South Africa's withdrawal from Namibia. The Cubans were only in Angola to defend the government against the UNITA rebel movement supported by South Africa. Nyerere promised to support the CG in their efforts to persuade SWAPO.[47]

After a very protracted journey from New York to Dar es Salaam, the Quintet was relieved to be able to fly the next four legs in a small US government aircraft. The Quintet duly arrived in Maputo on 23 November and was received by FM Chissano who was adamant that South Africa had to withdraw immediately and fully from Namibia since its presence there violated international law. It was not necessary to cite SWAPO's additional (and correct) argument that any residual South African troops would be an intimidating factor in the elections. In response to the CG's charge that the legalistic standpoint left no alternative but continued war, the Foreign Minister replied: "Of course, the overdue sanctions under Chapter VII!" SWAPO had made enough concessions by agreeing to elections and accepting the AG. Since the UN had recognised SWAPO as "sole and authentic representative" it had no need of elections. Control of SWAPO camps outside Namibia was out of the question until after the elections.

---

[47] DB 359 of 21.11.1977 from Dar es Salaam; President Nyerere 1968 on the right of self-determination, cf. Kunig, loc. cit. pp.386-388.

Chissano, in whose country Cubans were also stationed, significantly explained that any attempt to secure an Angolan guarantee for Cuban good behaviour was arrogant interference in Angola's sovereignty. At most, the CG could ask Angola not to disrupt an internationally recognised agreement once it had been reached. Fear of the Cubans was a transparent lie used as a pretext by Pretoria. The Five concluded from this hard-line approach that Mozambique was afraid that a compromise settlement for Namibia would weaken its radical position on Rhodesia.[48]

On 24 November, the Quintet held consultations with President Khama and Vice-President Masire in Gaborone. Both gave assurances that they supported the Namibia Initiative in every respect but also made it quite clear that their influence on SWAPO and other FLS was slight. Khama stressed that the CG's chances depended heavily on Angola's stance. In his opinion, President Neto found SWAPO's presence in Angola annoying since it repeatedly provided South Africans with excuses for violating the border and supporting UNITA. The CG urgently required a promise from Luanda – which it could present to Pretoria – that it would comply with an international agreement on Namibia. All the FLS, but especially Zambia, would like to see an end to SWAPO's military operations outside Namibia sooner rather than later.[49]

In Lusaka, President Kenneth Kaunda initially received the CG on 27 November for breakfast, which he began with a prayer. The meeting was later continued in the Cabinet room. In great earnest, Kaunda reproached the Five for their policy in Southern Africa, accusing them of going easy on Pretoria whilst abandoning the FLS and the liberation movements in their struggle.

> Through your passivity you have forced us to take arms from the Soviet Union and China. You have left us alone with your opponents and made

---

[48] DB 326 of 23.11.1977 from Maputo.
[49] DB 163 of 24.11.1977 from Gaborone.

them our allies. You have thus set yourselves in contradiction to the Christian ideas which you brought us. You do deals with the Anti-Christs Jan Smith and John Vorster.

Kaunda continued that he only took the Five's Initiative seriously because he had confidence in President Carter; not in his administration but in his "approach to life" which manifested itself above all in his new commitment to human rights issues. Allowing 1,500 South African troops to remain was problematical, but perhaps acceptable if this unit was concentrated at a very remote base near the South African border. 2,000 blue helmets were by no means sufficient. A long intermediary period up to the elections would be required, not only in SWAPO's interests but also to convert the Whites from their emotional prejudices to a better understanding of SWAPO. UN control of SWAPO in Zambia was not necessary. He would not tolerate the breach of an agreement accepted by all participants from his territory, such as infiltration of Namibia by SWAPO guerrillas.

However, Kaunda gave the overall impression that he wanted to avoid any current cause for criticism on the part of SWAPO.[50]

On 29 November, the Quintet arrived in Luanda where it was received by PM Lopo do Nascimento together with FM Paolo Jorge, his Under-Secretary Roberto de Almeida and Olga Lima, Head of the Political Directorate at the Foreign Ministry. The PM stated that Angola stood firmly by SWAPO and would continue to support its armed struggle should the negotiations fail. If an internationally accepted agreement were reached, Angola guaranteed that it would insist on full compliance and not permit any disturbances by SWAPO troops or other military forces from its territory. Luanda only wanted to examine the possibility of UN controls within Angola in the event of a convincingly proven need. The planned residual South African troop presence in Namibia was undesirable but acceptable if necessary. The PM estimated the UNTAG requirement at approx. 1,000

---

[50] DB 362 of 27.11.1977 from Lusaka.

civilian and 2,000 military forces. One key issue which had to be agreed with the FLS was the origin of the UN troops. Do Nascimento advocated a fully demilitarised zone (DMZ) north and south of the border with Namibia, thus revealing an aversion to UN supervision on the Angolan side. The project of a DMZ showed that SWAPO interests did not necessarily enjoy priority in Luanda.[51]

Departing from Luanda on 29 November and travelling on scheduled flights with notoriously unpredictable timetables, the Quintet eventually reached Lagos on 5 December, having taken the only possible route via Lusaka, Gaborone, Johannesburg (3 days transit in Pretoria) and Kinshasa. They were received by President General Olusegun Obasanjo on 7 December in the presence of FM Garba. Obasanjo began by stating that SWAPO's positions were decisive for Nigeria because SWAPO represented the Namibians, "though not all of them" (!). Since SWAPO primarily wanted free elections it ought to be possible to persuade them to accept a residual South African troop presence if the latter could be really neutralised. The Nigerian implied indirectly that he regarded SWAPO's military strength as meagre and exaggerated opposition to the settlement proposal as nonsense. At the same time, one also had to understand the interest of the Whites in maximum protection against a breach of the agreements. He wanted to talk to Nujoma. The threat to Angola from South African attacks and UNITA's support from Namibian territory had to be eliminated. Then the Cubans would be superfluous.[52]

Despite substantial reservations on the part of the FLS and Nigeria, the CG was not altogether disheartened. On the contrary, it believed that it was not unrealistic to hope that Nyerere and Obasanjo in particular – thanks to their influential position within the FLS – would make an impression on SWAPO. But one thing was definitely confirmed: despite their

---

[51]   DB 367 of 30.11.1977 from Lusaka.
[52]   Delegation report no. 14 of 7.12.1977 from Lagos.

distinct interest (only still doubtful in Maputo) in an early peaceful settlement, none of these six governments were prepared to approve an outcome that SWAPO had not fully accepted. It was also disappointing that neither Zambia nor Angola had given clear assurances on the important issue of UN control of SWAPO bases outside Namibia.

Just how sensibly the sequence of negotiating stages had been planned in New York became apparent to the CG when it nevertheless took advantage of the stopover in Lusaka to conduct a third round with SWAPO before travelling on to Lagos via South Africa. The meeting was held at the British Embassy on the afternoon of 27 November. Taking careful account of SWAPO's concerns, the CG made a thoroughly prepared attempt to shift Nujoma from his apodictic position, primarily on the issue of residual South African troops. Without success. The SWAPO president added a further explosive topic to this taboo by now demanding not 2,000 but 4,000-5,000 blue helmets. Even without South Africa's residual troops, no fair political process could be guaranteed with less UN presence because the whole of Namibia was contaminated with South African police and paramilitary. He questioned what results the Five had achieved with their "mediating role" since the second round. In his view, they were standing idly by while the AG registered voters without supervision and promoted the *Turnhalle* groups' election campaign which was already in full swing. – This problematical behaviour on the part of the AG was indeed undeniable. – The CG gained the impression that SWAPO had decided in advance to adopt this confrontational approach to counter any signs that the Five might be able to out-manoeuvre central SWAPO positions with the help of the FLS. The CG was therefore unable to gather any ammunition for the forthcoming trip to Pretoria. It was too early. However, the CG still expected that its FLS/Nigeria round would eventually have an effect on SWAPO.[53]

---

[53] DB 361 and DB 363 of 27.11.1977 from Lusaka. DB 367 of 29.111977 from Dar es Salaam.

As already mentioned, the CG travelled from Lusaka via Gaborone and Johannesburg to Pretoria for the fourth round with the South Africans. The Quintet met FM Botha and Under-Secretary Fourie informally in Fourie's private flat on 2 December 1977 and then officially at the Union Building on 3 December.

On 2 December, all Five – with divided roles – presented the main features of their own settlement proposal and the key points where further rapprochement between the conflicting parties was essential. The focus was on the number and UN supervision of South African soldiers who could remain in Namibia from the beginning of the election campaign until independence.[54]

Seated quite close to Botha, the German Quintet member (author) could clearly see that the Foreign Minister repeatedly consulted the documents in front of him which were patently copies – obtained by whatever means – of information telegrams from the Foreign Ministries in Dar es Salaam, Gaborone and Lusaka to their Embassies in the other FLS. These telegrams contained detailed information on the CG's talks of the previous few days in the respective capitals.

Botha and Fourie together delivered a long drawn-out sermon, stating that enough was now enough. The screw of unreasonable South African concessions was being tightened ever more relentlessly while nothing was being demanded of SWAPO, the UN favourites. The election date had definitively been set for the beginning of June 1978. The figure of 4,000 for South Africa's residual troops was final.

On 3 December, after long internal consultations with PM Vorster, the two men made the following proposal: South Africa could reduce its residual troops from 4,000 to 3,000 on the condition that 1,000 UN military observers were stationed in Angola north of the Namibian border in order to monitor SWAPO there. A further UN unit of no more than 1,000 blue

---

[54]   DB 541 of 3.12.1977 from Pretoria; DB 542 of 4.12.1977 from Pretoria.

helmets (previously 250) was to be deployed in Namibia as follows: 800 split into 3 groups and limited to certain locations along the northern border, namely 200 east of the Cunene estuary as far as Ruacana, 400 on the border from Ruacana to the Okavango River and 200 further east in the Caprivi Strip between the River Kwando and the Zambezi. The remaining 200 were to move freely around the whole of Namibia in order to observe the residual South African troops. South Africa insisted on retaining its 9 bases in Northern Namibia and occupying them with units of approx. 33 soldiers (1 platoon) each, 300 men in total. 1,400 South African combat troops would be concentrated in Oshivelo and 1,300 were required for logistical and technical support services.

It is worth giving such a detailed account of this proposal because both Botha's and Fourie's verbose reasoning and comments on the scattering of military forces in the North clearly, albeit perhaps unintentionally, revealed the following intentions:

(a) Since the South African side was convinced that any visible UN presence would work psychologically in SWAPO's favour, the UN military should disappear from the view of voters as far as possible, in other words as many as possible to Angola and the rest to the extreme northern periphery, apart from 200.

(b) The 9 South African bases in the North were secretly important to the South Africans for the following three main reasons: first, in order to suggest the "correct" election decision to voters in Ovamboland (where the majority lived); second, in order to discourage SWAPO attacks; and third, in order to monitor the UN military, thus putting paid to any UN support for SWAPO propaganda.

(c) Although they highlighted concerns about security in the North, Botha and Fourie made no further mention of the Cuban threat which had been so dramatised in the third round. The CG now knew once and for all that Pretoria believed just as little as they did in any serious Soviet-

Cuban intention of invading Namibia. At no point, neither now nor later, did South Africa consider Cuba's presence in Angola relevant to Namibia's security.

Pretoria's new numbers game did not improve the CG's mediation chances. It still faced South Africa's undisguised determination to secure an election victory for the *Turnhalle* elements, adopting a twin-track approach. Should the SC accept framework conditions favourable to this objective with the help of the CG, this would be the best way to avoid a SWAPO victory because it would have international blessing. Should the CG fail, however, the *Turnhalle* would be brought to power via an "internal solution" without SWAPO, regardless of the ensuing international isolation.[55]

Following the above-mentioned consultations in Lagos, the Quintet intended to return to New York on 7 December 1977. To their surprise, an instruction drafted by the British Foreign Secretary David Owen and agreed with his 4 CG counterparts arrived in Lagos from the 5 CG capitals: the Quintet was to return immediately to Lusaka and conduct a fourth SWAPO round there. Owen did not view the outcome of the talks in Pretoria as negatively as the Quintet. Although the Quintet considered this instruction pointless, if not highly risky for the continuation of the entire Initiative, they were now compelled to return to Lusaka on scheduled flights. There was no alternative to the route via Nairobi (!).

On 12 December, a new round of talks was held with SWAPO which lasted just 80 minutes. The CG presented Nujoma with a full report on the Pretoria meeting (leaving out the election date). It drew attention to the fact that South Africa would soon implement the "internal solution" if Nujoma stubbornly refused to make concessions and that SWAPO would

---

[55] Course of the fourth round with South Africa: DB 541 of 3.12.1977; DB 542, 544, 545 of 4.12.1977 – all from Pretoria; DB 3770 of 22.12.1977 from NY.

be held responsible for the failure of the international project. Nujoma stuck to his position that every last South African soldier had to leave Namibia before the political process started.

> SWAPO will not accept the presence of a single South African soldier at the beginning of the electoral campaign or thereafter.

He refused any further debate on this main topic, stating that it was pointless to discuss other elements of the settlement proposal until this SWAPO position had been accepted. The CG could pack up and go. Under African conditions, it was absurd to hope for helpful FLS/Nigeria influence on SWAPO after such a short time. In his report of 13 December, the German member of the Quintet notified the Federal Ministry of Foreign Affairs of their intention to return to New York with the words: "After 25 days ... the Five are beginning to believe in the end of the Anabasis".[56]

IX "What a disaster!"

By 23 December 1977, the CG in New York had drafted a "final settlement plan", once again based on SCR 385.[57]

Numerous detailed amendments were made to this still strictly confidential draft in the weeks that followed. One important improvement is worth noting: at Germany's suggestions, the CG dropped the recommendation that UNTAG's military component should consist of approx. 2,000 blue helmets. Rather than aggravating this controversial issue, the CG suggested instead that the SG call for the number of UNTAG personnel which his UN experts considered necessary.[58] The settlement plan

---

[56] DB 376 of 12.12.1977 from Lusaka; Anabasis (ancient Greek) = very long uphill march; title of a work by Xenophon (campaign by Cyrus the Younger against his brother Artaxerxes Mnemon).

[57] DB 3792 of 23.12.1977 from NY.

[58] DB 9 of 4.1.1978 from NY.

was finalised on 2 February 1978 and later went down in history virtually unchanged as the official "Proposal for a Settlement of the Namibia Situation" (S/12636) adopted by the SC in the famous Resolution 435 of 29 September 1978 (see Annex A).[59]

The Five were well aware that a decision would soon have to be reached in the SC. Several African States, along with the Soviets, were already prophesying that the Five would fail. Despite its various mediation efforts, the CG had not yet achieved sufficient rapprochement to ensure that the newly drafted proposal would have a smooth passage through the SC. Nothing more could be accomplished by continuing to deal with the two conflicting parties individually. A different negotiating strategy was now required: proximity talks.

The CG had realised that neither South Africa nor SWAPO wanted to be held responsible for the failure of a peaceful settlement. South Africa had to expect increasing Western pressure which would cause severe disruptions even if these measures were voluntary, i.e. below the threshold of binding chapter VII sanctions. SWAPO knew that the FLS and Nigeria were predominantly interested in the initiative succeeding and that the majority of the UN Africa Group followed them. The CG considered the moment was right to conduct concerted negotiations in New York and expose SWAPO to the direct and focussed influence of the Africans.

The decision in favour of proximity talks, which was developed within the CG during the period 20-23 December 1977, meant gathering representatives of the four key partners, namely South Africa, SWAPO, the FLS with Nigeria and the UN (SG), at a single location where each of them could negotiate separately with the five CG Foreign Ministers. The outcome of these meetings would determine whether some or all of the participants could then later sit down together around a single negotiating table. The CG proposed New York as the venue.

---

[59] Op. Para. 1 of SCR 435 (1978), approving the Five's letter of 10.4.1978 (S/12636) to the SC President.

The advantage of this arrangement was that, despite the confidentiality of the meetings, South Africa and SWAPO would be confronted with an unrelentingly aggressive and fairly knowledgeable global media presence. Neither would be able to seek refuge in the time delay which otherwise ensued until the opposite side reacted to each move. Both would be equally in the spotlight at a spectacularly high level (Foreign Minister), and South Africa would lose the comfortable framework of a "home game".[60]

After considerable effort, the CG managed to obtain the agreement of all the participants for the conference to be held on 10-12 February 1978. By common consent, the American UN Mission opposite the UN building on New York's First Avenue was to be the venue. As well as being close to the UN, it was also very suitable in terms of technical equipment and security. The Americans provided a large conference room, a press centre and two offices for each of the four CG Foreign Ministers. As a precaution, conference rooms were also reserved in the neighbouring United Nations Plaza Hotel, where the 5 Foreign Ministers, the South Africans and SWAPO would be staying.

In the first week of February, the CG had distributed the settlement proposal (Annex A) first to the SG, South Africa and SWAPO, then to the FLS, Nigeria and interested groups in Windhoek. Each recipient had been requested to treat the text as confidential. Secretary of State Cyrus Vance (USA), FM Hans-Dietrich Genscher (Germany), Foreign Secretary David Owen (Great Britain), FM Donald Jamieson (Canada) and FM Louis de Guiringaud (France) attended the proximity talks. South Africa was represented by FM Botha and SWAPO by Sam Nujoma. Participants from the FLS were UN Ambassador Elisio de Figueiredo for Angola, FM Mogwe for Botswana, presidential advisor Sergio Vieira for Mozambique, FM Siteke G. Mwale for Zambia and FM Benjamin Mkapa for Tanzania. FM Garba represented Nigeria. The African SC members Mauritius

---

[60]   DB 3735 of 20.12.1977 from NY; DB 3792 of 23.12.1977 from NY.

(represented by UN Ambassador Ramphul) and Gabon (UN Ambassador N'Dong) also took part. A request came from Windhoek for *Turnhalle* representatives and other political groups to participate. The CG did not refuse point-blank but made it clear that they would not be admitted to any official meetings. Those who did turn up in New York only received information on the current state of play from individual members of the core Quintet designated by the CG.[61]

On 10 February, the Quintet conducted preliminary talks with South Africa and SWAPO – attended in part by the 5 UN Ambassadors – in order to explain the settlement plan. The first official talks, chaired by Secretary of State Vance, were held on the morning of 11 February between the 5 Foreign Ministers and FM Botha, who again lamented theatrically that all concessions had so far come from South Africa. Yet he was still expected to make more. No clear signal could be obtained that he was prepared to give ground, especially regarding residual South African troops.

At the subsequent meeting chaired by FM Jamieson, Nujoma confirmed a fundamentally important move which he had already announced at the above-mentioned preliminary talks on 10 February to the CG's surprise and joy: for the first time, SWAPO accepted the 1,500 residual South African troops. Even though this concession was conditional on the South African troops stationed in Walvis Bay being counted towards the 1,500 and the UN-monitored assembly point in Namibia not being located in Grootfontein or Oshivelo but in Karasburg near the South African border, this breach of taboo signified an encouraging turn of events for the Five. The CG was certain that this was due to the influence of the FLS/Nigeria.

All those involved regarded these two meetings as moderate diplomatic overtures. Things would get tough at the next meetings.

After the 5 Foreign Ministers had conducted a friendly exchange of ideas with SG Waldheim over lunch and held a generally constructive meeting

---

61   The political groups from Windhoek and the names of their representatives are listed in DB 342 of 14.2.1978 from NY.

with the FLS, Nigeria and the African SC members Gabon and Mauritius, chaired by France, the stage was then set for the highly anticipated second act with FM Botha in the late afternoon. FM Genscher took the chair. He opened the meeting by presenting a text drafted by the Quintet. The first statement was that the CG had met with understanding among important African countries for its proposal to keep residual South African troops in Namibia with the proviso that this number was the absolute maximum and that a fair political process required a much higher number of military and civilian UNTAG personnel. South Africa could rely on the fact that the SG would be completely objective and impartial with regard to both the number and the origin of this personnel. His sole interest was in security and order – something which Pretoria also accorded high priority. Genscher virtually implored South Africa to seize the opportunity of a peaceful settlement which was now within reach. A rational and flexible approach to the outstanding differences would substantially improve South Africa's international position, whilst the otherwise inevitable denunciation in the SC was likely to result in extremely problematical measures for South Africa. Reading further from the prepared text, Genscher said in a friendly but matter-of-fact tone that it would be important

> that withdrawing South African troops would leave the territory and not be transferred to Walvis Bay ...

> The careful phrasing in the Western proposal that there will be no territorial claims reflected the fact that the Five did not share the South African position regarding Walvis Bay. It had appeared, this I like to report from the day's talks, that this question was generally taken very seriously by all parties.

Following Genscher's renewed exhortation to reconsider all the points mentioned and to reach a positive result in calm discussions the next day, Botha acted perplexed, rose from his seat and declared that he saw "no need to continue the talks" after what he had just heard. He would "return to South Africa immediately in order to report to his government." He briefly shook hands with each of the 5 dismayed Foreign Ministers and swept out of the conference room with his delegation. 'What a disaster!" exclaimed old James Murray. Downstairs at the exit to the US Mission, Botha retorted to the journalists encircling him: "Nothing to say."

Genscher succeeded in talking to Botha briefly in his hotel suite the following morning. Not very convincingly, Botha claimed that PM Vorster's instructions had left him no scope for movement towards the current settlement proposal. Everybody was now wondering why he had undertaken the long journey since the proposal had been submitted to him a week earlier in Pretoria. Genscher managed to reach an agreement that both Botha and the Five would tell the press: "the door has not closed."

Botha's walkout was a puzzling surprise. It was generally assumed that the clear rejection of South Africa's position on Walvis Bay had been the trigger. The British were absolutely certain of this.

The CG was aware from the beginning of the initiative that a dispute over the only deep-sea harbour on the Namibian coast was unavoidable. Pretoria claimed that the bay belonged to the Cape Province, while SWAPO insisted it was part of Namibia's territory. The conflict is not mentioned in SCR 385. Correspondingly, the Five did not encumber their written proposals with this issue. They consistently upheld the view that the conflict would have to be resolved later in negotiations between South Africa and an independent Namibia (which is what indeed happened after 1990). To explain the background:

Walvis Bay was seized by Great Britain in 1796 and treated as part of the Cape Colony from 1884. The Bay was incorporated into the Union of South Africa through the Union Act in 1910. Without changing this territorial status, the Union Parliament in Cape Town decided by Act no. 24 (1922) that the Bay should be placed under the administration of the mandated territory of South West Africa from 1 October 1922. It nevertheless remained part of the Cape Town constituency for parliamentary elections. With effect from 1 September 1977, South Africa once again transferred administration of Walvis Bay to the Cape Province, thus restoring the pre-1922 status quo. On 8 September 1977, PM Vorster publicly warned the Five not to question this status. "Walvis Bay is South African territory."[62]

The German delegation considered it highly unlikely that the CG's rejection of this position could have provoked Botha's outburst since the position reported by Genscher had already been clearly presented to the South Africans in the second and third rounds in 1977. A more plausible explanation was the shock that must have been caused by the sudden news – which Botha's people undoubtedly obtained over lunch – that SWAPO had accepted 1,500 residual South African troops. This surprise was enough to panic both Botha and Pretoria since, for the first time, the South Africans could no longer be certain that the Five would be thwarted by SWAPO. Botha fled in order to block the suddenly promising momentum towards a general consensus on the settlement proposal.

Despite considerable progress, the CG still faced difficult times ahead with SWAPO. This emerged as expected at the three following meetings conducted with Nujoma in the context of the proximity talks. After the opponent had decamped, the SWAPO President thought that, being a reasonable partner, he could now expect increased respect and understanding for his still rather sweeping criticism of the settlement plan. Under the chairmanship of the British Foreign Secretary David Owen, the 5 Foreign Ministers negotiated with him on the evening of 11 February. The Quintet met him for two further discussions on 13 and 16 February. At none of these meetings could SWAPO be persuaded to drop its main objections to the proposal. These were:

---

[62] DB 2055 of 15.9.1977 from NY; DB 2495 of 15.10.1977 from NY; DB 325 of 12.2.1978 from NY; DB 633 of 21.3.1978 from NY; written report no. 321 of 24.10.1977 from Windhoek to Section 320; Surface area of Namibia without Walvis Bay: 822,876 km^2; surface area of Walvis Bay: 1,124 km^2.

(a) The residual South African troops had to be monitored at a remote base in the South.

(b) Walvis Bay had to be explicitly designated as Namibian territory in the proposal.

(c) The AG was to be accountable to the UNSR. This also included command of the police which had to be disarmed.

(d) The UNSR had to decide in disputes over the release of political prisoners.

(e) UNTAG personnel: at least 1,000 civilians and at least 5,000 blue helmets. The proposal had to state this explicitly.

Despite his scepticism, Nujoma acknowledged the Five's role as honest broker several times. His intransigent position stemmed from mistrust of SA which had become entrenched through bitter experience.

The proximity talks[63] had brought progress with SWAPO and a more trusting and therefore more promising understanding with the FLS and Nigeria. Attempts by the five Cape Town Ambassadors in the following weeks to shift the South Africans towards a consensus, initially with Under-Secretary Fourie and then with FM Botha himself, produced only limited success. South Africa appeared more determined than ever to seek an "internal solution".[64]

---

[63] Course of the proximity talks: DB 208 of 30.1.1978; DB 285 of 8.2.1978; DB 312 and 322 of 10.2.1978; DB 323 of 11.2.1978; DB 325 and 326 of 12.2.1978; DB 336 of 13.2.1978; DB 342 of 14.2.1978; DB 368 of 16.2.1977 – all from NY.

[64] DB 345 of 14.2.1978 from NY; DB 38 of 17.2.1978 from Cape Town; DB 399 of 21.2.1978 from NY; DB 483 of 2.3.1978 from NY; DB 541 of 10.3.1978 from NY.

X First signs of concessions on both sides

No further progress could be made through negotiation. It was now a matter of mobilising the supreme instance on behalf of the CG proposal: the Security Council.

The Five continued polishing certain text passages until 13 March in order to manoeuvre them, SCR 385 permitting, as precisely as possible into the centre ground between South African and SWAPO dogmas. They then obtained the agreement of their respective governments to the final version (Annex A).[65]

This text was presented to the FLS, Nigeria and SC members Gabon and Mauritius in their capitals on 29 March 1978, to the South African government in Cape Town and SWAPO in Lusaka on 30 March and to interested political groups in Windhoek some days later.[66] SG Waldheim also received the text on 30 March. The CG stressed to him how essential it would be for UNTAG to proceed impartially and how understandable South Africa's mistrust was on this point in the light of several GA resolutions favourable to SWAPO and UN financial support for SWAPO. The Five were agreed that all this one-sidedness would eventually have to be eliminated. In compliance with an express wish of the CG, Waldheim issued a press statement emphasising that the UN had thoroughly proved its "competence and impartiality" in peace-keeping missions. Should the SC entrust the SG with a mandate for Namibia, everyone could rely on the UN carrying this out impartially and fairly.[67]

---

[65] DB 399 of 21.2.1978; DB 418 of 22.2.1978; DB 426 of 23.2.1978; DB 653 of 22.3.1978 – all from NY.

[66] DB 680 of 28.3.1978 from NY; DB 102 of 30.3.1978 from Cape Town.

[67] DB 665 of 24.3.1978 from NY; DB 710 of 30.3.1978 from NY. When FM Botha cast doubt on the "impartiality of the UN" on 30.3.1978, the five Ambassadors reacted as follows: "We urged him not to assume arbitrary action on the part of the Secretary General, reminding him that the Five were in any case themselves not going to walk away from the problem." (DB 102 of 30.3.1978 from Cape Town).

On 10 April 1978, the settlement proposal was published as official SC document S/12636.

When they made their *démarche* in Cape Town on 30 March, the five Ambassadors encountered an FM Botha who had meanwhile settled back into the dogma which was firmly established in the minds of virtually all apartheid leaders, namely that one could count on SWAPO's Moscow-backed opposition course, which mild FLS winds could hardly influence. Nujoma's remaining objections at the end of the proximity talks certainly encouraged this view. And SWAPO's subsequent actions seemed to confirm the dogma. PM Vorster initially attempted to shift internal responsibility for dealing with the SC plan onto the *Turnhalle* and other Namibians. Advised by the AG, DTA leader Mudge, some other groups and renowned Namibian church leaders did indeed assess the plan positively.[68] However, the Five insisted on the South African government taking responsibility. On 25 April, they were able to report that the South African Cabinet had accepted the settlement proposal that same day. The Prime Minister would be announcing this in Parliament at 4 pm.[69]

The previous day, a Special General Assembly (SGA) on Namibia had begun in New York at the initiative of the UN Africa Group. Since the CG had not received any positive signal from SWAPO, it had been unable to set up a prior session of the Security Council and obtain SC acceptance of the proposal. Consequently, this protective shield against the criticism of radical elements in the SGA was now missing. On 25 April, Ambassador Trojanovski of the Soviet Union thus preached that power should be transferred to SWAPO immediately; binding sanctions had to be imposed on South Africa; and a warning had to be issued about the manoeuvring of Western states allegedly seeking a settlement, since they were merely pursuing their own economic interests. As had already been the case at

---

[68]   DB 102 of 30.3.1978 from Cape Town; DB 766 of 4.4.1978 from NY.
[69]   DB 146 and DB 148 of 25.4.1978 from Cape Town.

the last regular GA, the SGA (3 May) concluded with a final document which designated SWAPO in no uncertain terms as the "sole and authentic representative" and called for "armed struggle with all means". The Five would have voted "No" on the substance, but in deference to their role as mediators they formally abstained without commenting on the substance, as they had done on all GA resolutions on Namibia since launching their initiative. The vote ended with 119 "Yes" votes and 21 abstentions. Greece, Spain and Portugal – EC candidates at the time – voted "Yes". Apart from the CG-Five, the other 6 EC countries plus Austria, Sweden, Iceland, Norway, Finland, Australia, New Zealand, Japan, Israel and Guatemala all abstained.[70]

An internal meeting of the FLS and Nigeria with Nujoma was held in the margins of the SGA on 26 April. Nujoma adopted such a negative position on the settlement proposal that a fierce argument broke out between him and FM Mkapa (Tanzania). Mkapa subsequently phoned President Obasanjo in Lagos; who instructed FM Garba (Nigeria) to arrange a meeting between Nujoma and Secretary of State Vance in Washington. Garba was to take part himself. Vance received the two immediately (on the morning of 27 April). Yet these discussions also failed to move the SWAPO leader who insisted on all the demands he had already presented at the proximity talks on 11 February.[71]

Notwithstanding its radical finale, the SGA obtained basic approval to the CG initiative from a clear majority, also within the Africa Group, albeit with numerous speakers criticising individual aspects of the settlement plan, in particular the non-inclusion of the Walvis Bay issue. The highlight was expected to be Nujoma's speech on the afternoon of 27 April. Quite a few were hoping to experience a "Yes" to the settlement plan. But not the Five, since they already had news from Washington. Nujoma adopted

---

[70]   DB 964 of 25.4.1978 from NY; DB 1044 of 3.5.1978 from NY.
[71]   DB 990 of 27.4.1978 from NY.

the most aggressive tone towards the CG since the initiative was launched. He was angry that the proposal had been presented to the SC without SWAPO's consent. He also spoke about the basis of trust being lost due to underhand CG arrangements with South Africa outside the settlement proposal. (In fact, nothing of the sort existed. SWAPO had construed a connection between rumours about a London conference of the Five and South Africa's early approval.) As in his meeting with Vance, Nujoma again listed all the SWAPO conditions of 11 February, thus virtually rejecting the CG's ideas. He did not exclude the possibility of further negotiations. The Five were quite despondent when they left. Trojanovski was beaming with delight.[72]

On 4 May, South African forces mounted an assault on the SWAPO refugee camp at Cassinga in southern Angola, killing more than 500, including many women and children. This brutal operation was irrelevant in military terms but politically useful for South Africa's goal of sabotaging the CG settlement. PM Vorster had given his Defence Minister, P.W. Botha, a notorious opponent of SCR 385, a completely free hand. It was not the SGA but this South African act of violence which propelled the Namibia Initiative into a crisis. It was now politically impossible for the FLS and Nigeria to exert visible pressure on SWAPO to drop their desired amendments to the substance of the settlement proposal. At Angola's request, a tough debate on Cassinga began in the SC on 6 May, which almost seemed like an interment of the Namibia Initiative. At all events, any chance of getting it through the SC in May was now gone.[73] A new round agreed with Nujoma on 3 May and scheduled to take place in New York on 8 May was cancelled by Nujoma himself in writing on 7 May:

> The SWAPO Central Committee which mandated our delegation in the talks has decided to urgently recall us in the light of the current pre-meditated and unprovoked aggression, through a massive armed invasion of the

---

[72] DB 1012 of 28.4.1978 from NY.
[73] DB 1074 of 6.5.1978 from NY; DB 1100 of 9.5.1978 from NY.

People's Republic of Angola by the fascist troops of racist South Africa, which is illegally utilizing Namibia for such criminal acts. As a result of this invasion hundreds of innocent Namibian men, women and children were killed and wounded and valuable property destroyed at Cassinga in southern Angola. Since the conclusion of the Security Council debate on the complaint of Angola against South Africa, I received further information about the devastation and destruction brought upon our refugee settlement by enemy forces. This situation requires our immediate presence there to appraise the circumstances of this barbaric act and to evaluate the extent of loss in human life and property.[74]

An FLS summit with SWAPO in Luanda on 10 and 11 June 1978 offered the first prospects of overcoming the stagnation.[75] As the appointed FLS spokesman, President Nyerere informed and advised the five Ambassadors in Dar es Salaam on 16 June as follows:

a) The summit had met the FLS concerns about a peaceful settlement better than expected. SWAPO had dropped virtually all its requested amendments, with the exception of the demand that the residual South African troops should not be stationed in Grootfontein or Oshivelo, but south of Windhoek. In his opinion, this was not Nujoma's last word.

b) SWAPO demanded an assurance from the SC that Walvis Bay belonged to Namibia's territory ("is an integral part").

c) There was no further talk of counting the South African contingent in Walvis Bay towards the troops.

d) The CG should first inform South Africa about the Luanda summit and seek approval on (a) and (b). It should then request a meeting with SWAPO in Luanda.[76]

---

[74]   DB 1085 of 8.5.1978 from NY.

[75]   DB 1373 of 6.6.1978 from NY.

[76]   DB 1449 of 12.6.1978 from NY.

On 28 June, FM Botha refused any change to the arrangements governing the locations of the residual troops. He also resisted the CG proposal that Pretoria should voluntarily renounce Oshivelo and retain only Grootfontein, provided that SWAPO accept the overall plan as it was.

Consequently, the Five required further movement from SWAPO. They upped the ante by giving Federal Chancellor Helmut Schmidt the CG mandate to try and obtain further assistance from President Obasanjo during his visit to Lagos on 26-28 June. The Federal Chancellor stressed that SWAPO was not motivated by security concerns but by completely understandable misgivings about the risk of voter intimidation. This could and must be avoided at both locations, Oshivelo and Grootfontein, through greater concentrations of UN troops. Obasanjo agreed and also did not contradict the Federal Chancellor's following comment on Walvis Bay:

> The Federal Government is prepared to endorse a positive and supportive statement in the Security Council in which the United Nations will make a firm commitment that Walvis Bay should be part of Namibia and that the international community will support efforts to have that territory returned to Namibia speedily.

On his own initiative, Helmut Schmidt used his subsequent visit to Lusaka on 29-30 June to make the same approach to President Kaunda and achieved a similarly positive reaction. The New York CG was encouraged and instructed the Five in Dar es Salaam to visit Nyerere and exploit the momentum. Nyerere recommended a final CG round with SWAPO in Luanda on 10-12 July, based on the unchanged settlement proposal. He attached great importance to Angola chairing this round, dispatched FM Benjamin Mkapa and called upon the other FLS also to send high-level representatives to Luanda.[77]

---

[77]   DB 1670 and 1671 of 30.6.1978; DB 1684 of 3.7.1978; DB 1688 of 5.7.1978; DB 1694 of 6.7.1978; DB 1724 of 13.7.1978 – all from NY. Federal Chancellor Helmut Schmidt also mentioned the Namibia Initiative in public in Lagos on 27.6. and in Lu-

It was the moment of truth for the Five. Conscious of this responsibility, the core Quintet travelled from New York to Luanda via Lisbon. Mervyn Brown had now replaced Murray as the British member. Angola had obviously decided to give this SWAPO round the gloss of a high-level international conference. On 9 July 1978, the Quintet were accorded a ceremonial welcome at Luanda airport by Deputy PM José Eduardo dos Santos and Pascual Luvualu, who dominated foreign policy in the MPLA Central Committee. They were accommodated in the State Guest House and received first-class protocol attention at all times. The conference was held in the town hall's large meeting room, at the time the only representative conference room that had not fallen victim to the war of liberation and the still visible vandalism caused by the Portuguese colonial masters in their attempt to destroy as much as possible when they departed in 1975. The opening session, chaired by Luvualu and dos Santos on 10 July, was attended by the CG and a 16-strong SWAPO delegation led by President Nujoma, as well as FM Mkapa and Mark Shona, President Kaunda's influential adviser in the FLS, together with government representatives from Mozambique and Botswana.[78]

In his introductory appeal, Luvualu left no doubt about the importance and urgency of an agreement for Angola, by evoking the opportunity:

> ... for seeking – with good will and the combined efforts of the five Member Countries of the Security Council, the Front Line Countries and SWAPO – a just and definitive solution which is in keeping with the most legitimate interests of the Namibian people and of all peace-loving peoples of this region of the African Continent.

During the negotiations, which were conducted only between the CG and SWAPO, but which the CG repeatedly interrupted to spend long breaks

---

saka on 29.6.1978 (cf "The Visit of the Federal Chancellor to Nigeria and Zambia." Federal Press and Information Office Bonn, 1978, p. 29 and p. 55).

[78] In addition to Nujoma, the SWAPO delegation heads were Theo-Ben Gurirab and Hidipo Hamutenya.

with the FLS in order to keep SWAPO reined in, Nujoma stubbornly upheld his familiar objections to the settlement plan. It was not until the evening of 12 July that the CG managed to wrest a resigned nod from the evasive SWAPO leader, which the CG immediately bagged as a resounding "yes" to the long-sought promise that SWAPO would demand no further amendments to the text in the SC.

The pre-condition to that nod had been an extremely difficult agreement on a separate SC Resolution on Walvis Bay. SWAPO had not insisted on the wording "as an integral part" but had rejected the statement that it should be incorporated into Namibian territory through "negotiations" or by "agreement". Such a concession to Pretoria's current legal presumption went too far; instead of announcing radical SC measures, the initiative was left to the South Africans; everyone knew that Pretoria was resisting negotiations. Thanks to the crucial help of FM Mkapa and Mark Shona behind the scenes, the following had been achieved in the night of 11 to 12 July:

The CG did not insist on its proposal: "The Security Council decides to lend its full support to the initiation of steps necessary on the reintegration of Walvis Bay and independent Namibia." This sentence should rather end with the words "... of steps necessary to ensure early reintegration of Walvis Bay into Namibia." The tug-of-war thus ended with agreement on the text which eventually became the core sentence (op. para.2) of the Security Council's Walvis Bay Resolution of 27 July 1978 (SCR 432). The Five quickly made it clear to everyone concerned that "necessary steps" meant nothing other than negotiations between South African and Namibia. SWAPO refrained from voicing any opposition.

At the final meeting of the totally exhausted participants, SWAPO did not allow the CG to include a simple message of success in the final joint communiqué stating that SWAPO had agreed to the settlement plan. Instead, the key sentence merely stated:

During two days of frank and cordial discussion certain points in the proposal of the five powers were clarified and the two delegations accordingly
agreed to proceed to the U.N. Security Council thus opening the way to
an early internationally acceptable settlement of the question of Namibia.

Nevertheless, the German in the Quintet could not resist giving a true and
graphic account of the outcome in his report to the Federal Ministry of
Foreign Affairs in Bonn:

> After concluding remarks by Luvualu, McHenry and Nujoma, the FLS
> representatives openly demonstrated their relief and applauded the result.
> While FM Mkapa performed a joyful pirouette before the eyes of the as-
> tonished SWAPO delegates, each of the western Five and then also Nu-
> joma were audibly kissed on both cheeks by the old, dignified Luvualu.[79]

The following day, FM Genscher sent a telegram congratulating the Quintet and thanking them for their tireless commitment.[80]

XI Success – but no reason for celebration

The Five had indeed achieved something remarkable which most UN
members had thought unlikely even shortly before: the majority in the
SC, including all the African members, were preparing to adopt a Western
plan on southern Africa despite bitter UN condemnations of the West for
its relations with South Africa and despite considerable Soviet influence in
the region. To that extent, the Five were now on secure ground.

South Africa by no means inspired the same degree of confidence. The
"internal solution" had remained an alternative for Pretoria. The CG was
aware that, in addition to South Africa's unacceptable interest in continuing to dominate Namibia and protect the apartheid system, there were also
legitimate South African reservations about the UN settlement plan which
weakened its powers of persuasion: the symptoms of a UN bias in favour

---

[79]   DB 1733 of 14.7.1978 from NY.
[80]   DE 3492 of 13.7.1978 from Bonn (Section 320).

of SWAPO and the suspicion that SWAPO would establish a radical anti-White dictatorship. "Impartiality" and rule-of-law guarantees were tasks that the CG would inevitably have to tackle. All Five would also have to confront these issues at home in their domestic politics.[81]

On 27 July 1978, the SC adopted the "Mandate Resolution" SCR 431 by 13 votes to none, with 2 abstentions (Soviet Union and Czechoslovakia). China's assent came as a surprise since Beijing had never previously participated in votes on peace-keeping measures. The Resolution took note of the Western settlement proposal, requested the SG to appoint a Special Representative and to submit at the earliest possible date a plan for the implementation of the settlement proposal in accordance with SCR 385. Without amending the text agreed in Luanda, the SC then unanimously adopted the "Walvis Bay Resolution" SCR 432. As the published record of SC session S/PV.2082 shows, FM Genscher, Owen, Vance, de Guiringaud and Botha all attended in person. As previously agreed, SG Waldheim took the floor first and announced that he was appointing Martti Ahtisaari (Finland) as the UNSR.

On 29 August, the SG caused quite a commotion when he presented the plan (S/12827) requested under SCR 431, demanding 7,500 persons for the military element of UNTAG and 1,560 persons for the civilian component. Assuming a one-year UNTAG operation, he estimated costs of US$ 300 million. Due to the time required for this UNTAG build-up, elections could not be scheduled until the end of April 1979.

Just two days later, Under-Secretary Fourie reproached the CG on a visit to New York, claiming that the figure of 7,500 came as a complete surprise to South Africa and was unacceptable. This was a "highly emotional and political issue". In substance, FM Botha also upheld this position on 1 September. Although its expectations that the CG would be thwarted by SWAPO blocking tactics had been dashed, Pretoria was

---

[81] DB 1017 of 1.5.1978 from NY; DB 1860 of 4.8.1978 from NY; DB 1929 of 18.8.1978 from NY.

still firmly convinced that it could deal with elections under the CG plan with a maximum of 1,000 UNTAG personnel for which South Africa was prepared and that, despite their presence, it possessed sufficiently reliable control and intimidation machinery to show "its" Blacks how they had to vote. Now to be confronted by the SG with figures of 7,500 plus 1,560 was a serious blow. It swept away any prospect of victory by the Turnhalle forces. Hence PM Vorster's immediate decision to pre-empt the time-consuming build-up of such a UN force by scheduling elections for the end of 1978 on his own authority. The German Embassy in Pretoria reported this on 31 August.[82] On 19 September, the SA Cabinet followed the PM's instructions and decided: elections on 20-24 November. The AG arranged for a postponement on technical grounds until 4-8 December 1978.[83]

The Foreign Ministers of the Five, who were in New York for the GA and in anticipation of the decisive SC session on Namibia, met for consultations on 25 September. They were dismayed. FM Genscher suggested that all five Foreign Ministers should travel to Pretoria together in mid-October and make the new South African Prime Minister aware of the consequences of such a breach of promise. He added that the Five also had to be prepared to issue "a credible threat". The New York Quintet, which was present but had not been consulted about this visit project, was surprised.[84]

The news from Pretoria hung like a dark cloud over the historic SC session of 29 September 1978 at which SCR 435 was adopted. It was this Resolution (cf. Annex B) which produced the SC's express approval of

---

[82]   DB 417 of 31.8.1978 from Pretoria.

[83]   DB 466 of 20.9.1978 from Pretoria; DB 492 of 27.9.1978 from Pretoria. (For more on South Africa's speculation about SWAPO's blockading position, cf. DB 271 of 14.7.1978 from Pretoria; on the CG's reaction to the South African Cabinet decision of 19.9.1978, cf. DB 2239 of 20.9.1978 from NY.)

[84]   DB 2302 of 25.9.1978 from NY; DB 2381 of 28.9.1979 from NY; DB 2407 of 30.9.1978 from NY. On Genscher's SC speech, cf. the author in ZEI loc. cit. pp. 232/233.

the Western plan and, despite later dangerous challenges, remained the foundation of the final Namibia Settlement (for more on the SC debate cf. records S/PV.2087 and 2088). Once again the vote was 13 to none in favour. China did not take part in the vote but later issued a statement that Peking would pay nothing towards UNTAG. The Soviet Union and Czechoslovakia abstained. The Kremlin had serious reservations about the SC giving the go-ahead to a plan by 5 NATO states. But the Kremlin was in the same dilemma as Pretoria: it too had always been certain that "its" FLS and SWAPO "brothers" would never do a deal with "neo-colonialists and apartheid accomplices". This is why it had constantly reiterated that southern Africa belonged to the Africans; what really counted was what they and, in particular, the liberation movements wanted. So how could they now justify a veto?

B 1979 to 1982: Despite Pretoria's delaying tactics, two milestones of confidence building

I Carnival in Pretoria

With their spontaneous travel project, the five Foreign Ministers had created a far more serious dilemma for the CG. Everyone at the UN as well as the world press[85] were certain that such a high-calibre delegation would naturally put P.W. Botha under sufficient pressure to implement SCR 435 correctly, i.e. abandon the December elections. The CG had indeed received instructions from its five Foreign Ministers to draw up proposals in New York, together with high-ranking officials from the five Foreign Ministries and economic experts, for measures that were to sound threatening enough to induce Pretoria to see reason. After four days in closed session, the Quintet reached agreement with the delegates from their respective capitals that the negative consequences of sanctions for the national economies of the Five would be less damaging than the negative political consequences of failure in Pretoria (loss of confidence among the African countries, increased pressure for sanctions in the SC, intensification of the armed struggle, growth of Moscow's influence). They offered a range of selective, rapid and targeted measures which would hit the elite where it hurt most, e.g. an air and sea blockade, an oil embargo, a ban on lending, foreign exchange, banking and foreign trade deals. But their main argument was that the "credible threat" had to reinforce the "stern action" signal of 7 April 1977 and focus attention on the specific risk that western resistance to sanctions under Chapter VII could no longer be guaranteed.[86]

---

[85] DB 535 of 11.10.1978 from Pretoria (regarding *FAZ*); *Der Spiegel* 1978, no. 42 (pp.140-142), no. 43 (p.162).

[86] DB 2417 of 2.10.1978 from NY; DB 2483 of 5.10.1978. Knowing how delicate the material was for everyone back at home, the Quintet had dug deep into the UN past

Things turned out very differently.

Secretary of State Vance, FM Genscher, Foreign Secretary David Owen and FM Donald Jamieson (Canada) as well as Under-Secretary Stirn (France) met PM P.W. Botha and FM Roelof Botha, constantly assisted by their experts, at the Union Building in Pretoria on 16-18 October 1978. At Owen's suggestion, the western Foreign Ministers had decided shortly before the first session began to exclude all their advisers, including the New York Quintet – to the obvious amusement of their South African counterparts. In the conference room, the Bothas relied on the sound support of AG Steyn, Under-Secretary Fourie, Defence Minister General Malan and several experts from the Foreign Ministry[87].

In his introductory comments, the PM spoke in detail about South Africa's historical contributions since World War I to the defence of western values and western interests (addressed to Genscher, e.g. referring to South African assistance during the Berlin blockade of 1948/49); about the vital Western links with South Africa (e.g. the Cape Route for oil supplies); and

---

and come up with a Korea document from 1952 as a protective precedent: Report of the Collective Measures Committee 1952, Doc.Ga.Official Records: 7th Session, supplement No. 17 (A/2215) page 20, cf. also DB 2552 of 8.10.1978 from NY; DB 2573 of 9.10.1978 from NY; DB 2586 of 10.10.1978 from NY (The line taken here was emphatically advocated by the German in the Quintet but only reluctantly accepted by the German officials from Bonn).

[87] For more on this exclusion, cf. the author in ZEI loc.cit. p.233, footnote 25: Jamieson later told the Canadian media that "hair-splitters" and "nit-pickers" should keep out of high politics. Amusingly illogical on this subject cf. also Vance, loc.cit. p.309. For a rather tough stance: McHenry in Weiland/Braham loc.cit. p.35: "The foreign ministers did what foreign ministers always do: they act on the basis of very little knowledge. They do not get themselves fully briefed and are inclined to consider what staff say as bureaucratic nit-picking when in fact it often involves fundamental issues. Two foreign ministers, the British and the Canadian, decided it was all a political matter to be solved by politicians, so they excluded the Contact Group. What you had were five ministers and the South African team, who took them to lunch!" – Apart from the German member of the Quintet, Genscher's excluded delegation consisted of Klaus Kinkel, Helmut Müller, Leonhard Kremer, Karl Lewalter and Jürgen Sudhoff. Only the German Foreign Ministry interpreter, Ms Gisela Niederste-Ostholt, was allowed to remain with FM Genscher.

about the current expansion of Soviet influence on the African continent. He insisted on the right of Namibians to say "No to Marxism" in December. South Africa was a well-ordered country. The Foreign Ministers should stay for a long time and definitely visit Cape Town.

Vance, Genscher and Owen reminded him of the seriousness of the situation. By obstructing the Namibia Initiative, South Africa was playing into Moscow's hands. Admittedly, the liberation movements were currently close to the Soviets, but this was largely a result of the West's failure in its dealings with them. Genscher predicted that early elections would trigger the severance of all support from the African countries. The Five would reject such elections and treat them as null and void.

Botha registered the fact that Genscher did not threaten any tougher measures as a reaction by the Five and adopted an increasingly challenging tone during this introductory phase. Troop numbers of 7,500 were "contrary to the agreement". The Five had painted the SG a false picture with regard to an acceptable figure. Why so many? South Africa had been led to assume parity between UN and South African troops. Nothing would persuade Pretoria to forego the December elections. If that was what the West wanted, it meant the end of negotiations with the CG and the UN. It was important to ensure that an elected Namibian body, instead of Pretoria, would take up the negotiations after the elections.

The five Foreign Ministers were also seated next to P.W. Botha, FM Botha and General Malan at the separate main table for the dinner on 16 October, whilst the accompanying CG members were relegated to the distant "children's table". By now, the PM was so sure of himself that he scornfully made fun of the current uncertainties which Vance, Owen and Jamieson faced regarding re-election back at home. Just as he was about to affront the German FM in the same way, Genscher thumped the table so hard that he set all the glasses dancing and declared that the governments of the Five at least had a legitimate democratic basis, unlike South Africa where four-fifths of the population were not permitted to participate in elections. Moreover, the PM would be well advised to reckon with the German Foreign Minister for a long time to come. With that, Genscher left the room before the dinner ended, followed by the other four. In confusion, the Bothas rushed after them to the adjacent room and resumed the conversation in pacifying tones. P.W. Botha stated that the December elections would be conducted according to democratic rules. SWAPO would be free to participate. South Africa could manage on its own, but would like to be understood internationally. The Five could send observers. If they hindered these correct elections, they would have to bear the consequences. The UN was obviously biased in favour of SWAPO, as was quite apparent from the "sole and authentic" Resolution. The Waldheim report dealt with the police and troop numbers in a way which deviated from the settlement plan. The Five had broken their promise several times – for instance over the AG /UNSR relationship and the Walvis Bay issue. The five Foreign Ministers reacted uncertainly to such false allegations, later repeated several times by FM Botha, which would have been inconceivable if their experts had been with them. The PM continued by saying that the Namibian people only trusted Pretoria and that this trust was more important to his government than that of the Five who intended to deny recognition of the elections for SWAPO's sake. "We were not frightened by the arms embargo. I would love to show you our arms factories." When Vance attempted to explain the connections with regard to troop numbers, the PM interrupted him: "Accept our approach or you will be on the losing side in Africa!" When he remarked that the discussion was now becoming absurd, the French Under-Secretary Stirn was told that he was free to leave. The French did not keep their word, as the arms embargo had shown. South Africa had invested huge sums in Namibia. Pretoria would present any government there, even if it consisted of the DTA, with the bill for all that and obtain payment by force if necessary. When the Five insisted that the elections were not compatible with SCR 435, the PM referred to South Africa's sovereignty. Nobody should imagine that

SWAPO was in control here. Under no circumstances would the elections be postponed for the UN's sake.

P.W. Botha concluded his strident monologue, which was shambolic like everything else at this highly political meeting, by renewing his appeal to the five Foreign Ministers that they had to see more of the country in order to understand South Africa. They were invited to undertake an air excursion with him to Cape Town.

On 17 October, Foreign Minister Botha continued the talks in the PM's absence. He conceded that the Five had been able to dispel some, though unfortunately not all of South Africa's concerns about the Waldheim report. There was no reason why the December elections should not be followed by further elections with UN involvement. But a date for that could only be agreed after the December elections with the then elected Namibian representatives. Genscher contradicted this. SCR 435 left no scope for internal interim elections. Owen spontaneously asked whether the election of a constituent assembly scheduled for December might not be restricted instead to the election of an "advisory body", whose function could be immediately suspended. FM Botha protested against such a manoeuvre. He derived distinct satisfaction from the fact that the British Foreign Secretary was already talking as if he had come to terms with the December elections taking place.

There followed an internal discussion between the five Foreign Ministers and their delegation members which removed any remaining hope among the latter that the debacle could still be avoided. They had to acknowledge that none of the Foreign Ministers had been authorised by their respective governments to play the "stern action" card. Owen repeated his idea of an "advisory body", which the Quintet unanimously regarded as counter-productive. In agreement with the Quintet, Genscher insisted on strict adherence to SCR 435, the beginning of UNTAG preparations and setting a fixed date for UN-controlled elections. But it became clear that he too was becoming resigned to internal interim elections when he failed to contradict the conclusion drawn by Jamieson and Owen that the Five would probably first have to "get over the elections". Then it would be a matter of tough insistence on SCR 435, if necessary by threatening sanctions.

When the session resumed under the chairmanship of FM Botha, the South Africans surprisingly circulated a draft of "interim conclusions". The Five responded to the references it contained to December elections by merely reiterating that they would regard them as null and void, whilst expressing interest in a joint final statement. Genscher warned that it was now time to reach agreement on how the UN plan was to be pursued after internal elections that were incompatible with SCR 435. To which Botha replied that they had apparently reached a dead-end; he saw no hope of an agreement; South Africa would probably have to go it alone. Vance considered this low point at the end of the meeting an appropriate moment to comment that if nothing better emerged on 18 October, the Five would decline the invitation to Cape Town. This was obviously the only "stern action" threat the Ministers could think of.

On 18 October, FM Botha declared that at no time since adoption of the settlement proposal had South Africa opposed the preparation of UNTAG and the arrival of the UNSR for consultations with the AG. However, the difficulties caused by the SG's report had led to delays. The December elections were a prerequisite for the further implementation of the CG's plan because only the elected Namibian "leaders" would have the authority to give the AG instructions regarding the timing of later elections under SCR 435 to be agreed with the UNSR. This showed that even the Five could not achieve their objective without a certain recognition of the December elections. No transition process could be initiated without a partnership between the UN and the "leaders".

After the Five had insisted that those elected under such circumstances could never be recognised as representative, all that remained was to discuss the text of a joint statement. All three ensuing drafts had one thing in common: they contained clarifications on the interpretation of the Wald-heim report and the further procedure between the UNSR and the AG which in no way plausibly justified the presence of five Foreign Ministers. This could have been done unspectacularly at working level in New York; a simple letter would have sufficed to express the Five's opinion on the nullity of the elections. In two drafts, the failure of the Foreign Ministers' mission was concealed in the statement that the Five would regard the De-cember elections as "null and void". By contrast, a draft formulated largely by the German side at least contained the passage:

> The five Foreign Ministers stated with regard to the planned December elections that they would seriously put at risk the implementation of their proposal. They confirmed that the process leading to independence has to be in conformity with Security Council Resolution 435 in all its parts. They are convinced that there is no need for any internal measures af-fecting the electoral process which would be incompatible with Security Council Resolution 435 and will not recognize any such measures, and therefore dissociate themselves from any unilateral action.

No agreement was reached. The five Foreign Ministers eventually left it to the South Africans to have the South African Cabinet decide after their departure which of the three drafts would constitute the joint declaration. At the end of this procedure – unique in diplomacy in the experience of all those accompanying the Foreign Ministers – the passage quoted above was dropped. Point 5 of the final declaration merely stated:

> The five Foreign Ministers stated with regard to the unilateral elections in December that they saw no way of reconciling such elections with the proposal which they put forward and which the Security Council has en-dorsed. Any such unilateral measure in relation to the electoral process will be regarded as null and void.[88]

---

[88] At South Africa's insistence a version (not as delivered) of the PM's opening state-ment of 16.10.1978, the text of the joint communiqué and the text of a unilat-eral South African Final Declaration were published as UN Document S/12900 of 19.10.1978. A unilateral Declaration by the Five appeared as UN Document S/12902 of 19.10.1978.

Assembled for a farewell in P.W. Botha's office, the five Foreign Ministers had to endure his accusation that they were breaking off the negotiations and were subjected to a torrent of words from the PM who permitted no interruption until FM Genscher picked up his files and dropped them with a crash onto the table. Genscher refused to tolerate the insinuation that the Five were breaking off the negotiations. This was due solely to the hosts' intransigence.

The Five then calmly departed.[89]

II With their backs to the wall

In New York the "Gang of the Five" now had their backs to the wall. All the African countries reacted with profound disappointment, often combined with reproachful acrimony. There was talk of turning away from the CG and focusing more on the armed struggle and coercive measures under Chapter VII. If the December elections were indeed held, that would spell the end of the SCR 435 project. Since there was not yet even a date for UN elections and full approval of the Waldheim report had not been achieved, what was the point of sending the UNSR to Windhoek? The SC strongly condemned South Africa's election project in SCR 439 of 13 November 1978.[90]

The internal elections without SWAPO for a constituent assembly with 50 seats were in fact held in Namibia on 4-8 December 1978. The DTA attained 82,2% (41 seats) whilst the right-wing conservative Action Front for the Retention of Turnhalle Principles (AKTUR) won 11,9% (6 seats).

---

[89]   The author's information on the ministerial talks in Pretoria on 16-18 October 1978 is based on his talks on this topic with FM Genscher during the days in Pretoria and on 17.1.2001 in Berlin, also with Under-Secretary Fourie in Pretoria on 28.6.1993, as well as on information received from Ms Niederste-Ostholt with FM Genscher's approval on 18 and 19.10.1978.

[90]   DB 2783 of 24.10.1978; DB 2826 of 26.10.1978; DB 2892 of 31.10.1978; DB 2907 of 1.11.1978; DB 134 of 23.1.1979 – all from NY.

South Africa's claim that 80,3% of those eligible to vote had participated in the elections was far from the truth. Many Blacks and in particular many "Ovambos" (almost half the total Black population, predominantly SWAPO supporters) resisted the pressure to take part in the elections or cast invalid ballot papers.[91]

Pretoria was evidently becoming more ensconced than ever in a twin-track approach: intensifying efforts to consolidate a solution without UN or SWAPO involvement on the one hand, whilst also signalling a constant readiness to stage endless consultations with the CG, the SG and the UNSR with the aim of remaining beyond the scope of Chapter VII and eventually, above all by including the DTA in all the various negotiations, manoeuvring the internal solution somehow into an international one.[92]

In January 1979, Ahtisaari began preparations for the UNTAG operation. No one imagined at the time that more than 10 years would elapse before it was implemented. As mentioned in the introduction, this account only deals with UNTAG developments to the extent that they had a major influence on the CG negotiating process. This included the issue of which countries were to provide the UNTAG personnel since South Africa would be opposed to any forces suspected of a biased pro-SWAPO position. As already described, there were aspects of UN behaviour which raised legitimate doubts about their impartiality. Back in January 1979, the CG had discussed among themselves and in consultation with the UNSR the fact that the problem of "impartiality" would have to be faced.[93]

---

[91] DB 736 of 15.12.1978 from Pretoria; Brenke loc.cit., p.24.

[92] DB 3702 of 15.12.1978 from NY (Extract from CG message to the South African government: "The decision to hold the elections and talk of a constituent assembly has from NY come close to wrecking the five's initiative."); DB 3837 of 23.12.1978 from NY; DB 3838 of 26.12.1978; SC Documents S/12938 of 24.11.1978; S/12950 of 2.12.1978; S/12983 of 23.12.1978 Annex I and Annex II.

[93] For more on UNTAG cf. footnote 3 above; CG dealing with "impartiality" cf. DB 41 of 9.1.1979 from NY.

The SG had misgivings about deploying UNTAG as long as South Africa and SWAPO confronted him with conflicting interpretations of the settlement plan (Annex A), primarily with regard to sub-paragraph 8a which reads, "... restriction of South African and SWAPO armed forces to base." It had not been resolved just where these bases for SWAPO should be. However, there had never been any doubt that, for SWAPO fighters within Namibia, the UNSR would designate assembly points in Namibia whilst Angola and Zambia, in co-operation with the UN liaison offices, were to assume responsibility for ensuring a moratorium by the SWAPO units in their countries, (cf. sub-paragraph 12 in Annex A).

South Africa had always insisted that SWAPO's presence within Namibia was only temporary and only in a limited number of guerrillas without fixed bases. Although the CG had never confirmed this in writing, the CG, the FLS and the UN Secretariat had always considered it realistic in view of South Africa's omnipresent military controls. Pretoria now called for genuine UNTAG supervision in Angola and Zambia, knowing that Luanda and Lusaka would not agree. For their part, SWAPO maintained (unjustly) that the settlement plan guaranteed them bases within Namibia. Nujoma now approached the Secretariat with the astonishing demand that there had to be three weeks between the date of the ceasefire and its entry into force; during these 3 weeks SWAPO would be permitted to transfer 2,500 armed combatants from Angola/Zambia to bases within Namibia.[94]

The CG refused to enter into new negotiations with the conflicting parties. Instead, it suggested to the SG that he should now document his interpretation as the authoritative version in an official report to the SC. It advised him to ignore the new SWAPO positions and merely confirm that SWAPO fighters – if there were actually any in Namibia at the beginning of the ceasefire – should either return to their camps in Angola/Zambia

---

[94] DB 291 and 293 of 14.2.1979; DB 305 of 15.2.1979 – all from NY.

or disarm and take part peacefully in the elections or be confined to bases within Namibia under UN supervision. The SG then published supervision rules for Namibia, Angola and Zambia along these lines in sub-paragraphs 11, 12 and 13 of his SC Report of 26 February 1979 (S/13120).[95]

It is worth going into these developments in such detail because South Africa subsequently devised the completely unjustified suspicion that the UN had secretly accepted the plan regarding 2,500 SWAPO fighters in agreement with the CG. On the other hand, there were concerns within the CG itself that the SG's report might be misinterpreted by SWAPO as an invitation to infiltrate shortly before the ceasefire came into force. Ten years later, the drama of 1 April 1990 focused the spotlight on this issue once again.[96]

South Africa's polemic against the SG's report, but also uncertainties about the specific nature of SWAPO supervision in Angola and Zambia, mutual reservations about the origin of some envisaged UNTAG troop units, South African military strikes on SWAPO positions in neighbouring countries – all these dangers, which threatened to completely destroy the climate of understanding and push the CG/UN goal of a ceasefire beyond reach, prompted the Five to propose proximity talks for the second time at CG Foreign Minister level, once again in New York. They were scheduled to begin on 18 March 1979.[97]

Participants for the Five were Secretary of State Vance, Foreign Secretary Owen, Foreign Minister Jamieson and, representing their Foreign Ministers, Under-Secretary Günther van Well (Germany) and Under-Secretary Stirn (France).

After discussions with the SG and a hearing of the internal parties, which caused considerable displeasure among the Africans, meetings were

---

[95] DB 316 of 17.2.1979; DB 331 of 20.2.1979; DB 343 of 22.2.1979 – all from NY.

[96] DB 385 of 27.2.1979 from NY; DB 386 of 28.2.1979 from NY.

[97] Documents for the second proximity talks: DB 517 of 15.3.1979; DB 526 and 529 of 16.3.1979 – all from NY.

held with the FLS and Nigeria on 19 and 20 March which were friendly on the whole. The latter opposed South Africa's idea of concentrating all SWAPO fighters in Angola and Zambia in bases to be announced. The risk was too great that South Africa would exploit the opportunity to destroy SWAPO's entire military wing. Surprisingly, the FLS arranged for the SWAPO delegation led by Vice-President Muyongo to be included in the ministerial talks on 20 March. They then stated: SWAPO outside Namibia was only to be controlled by the respective FLS; the UN's role had to be limited to UNTAG liaison offices. SWAPO would give a firm promise not to deploy any more armed fighters into Namibia after the ceasefire. Troops present in Namibia prior to the ceasefire had to be confined to camps by UNTAG.

The later meeting with FM Botha revealed that South Africa stuck to its patently unviable positions that complete UNTAG control of SWAPO in the neighbouring countries had to be guaranteed and that there must be no SWAPO bases in Namibia under any circumstances. Botha insisted on elections in September 1979, which would have left UNTAG far too little time for preparation. After the wretched performance by the five Foreign Ministers in Pretoria in October, the Bothas no longer thought it necessary to conceal the fact that they intended to block implementation of SCR 435 for the time being and derive benefits for the "internal solution". Without demanding anything in return, the Five had obliged them by receiving the internal parties, and above all DTA leader Dirk Mudge, for the first time at FM level – in response to a British proposal and against the advice of the German side. Harmonious consultations, which continued at the level below the CG heads of delegation with SWAPO, the FLS, the SG and the UNSR right up to 22 March, could not alter the fact that these proximity talks had to be considered a failure due to South Africa's blockade of the settlement plan.[98]

---

[98] Course of the second proximity talks: DB 541 and 545 of 19.3.1979; DB 552 and 553 of 20.3.1979; DB 567 and 569 of 22.3.1979; continued South African resist-

III Two break-through attempts in Geneva

Pretoria scheduled the opening of the "Constituent Assembly" in Windhoek for 2 April. In a sarcastic analogy to the Rhodesia problem caused by Ian Smith's "Unilateral Declaration of Independence", the short-hand in New York for the Windhoek phantoms was "creeping UDI".

There followed months of repeated attempts by the CG to overcome the blockade. This included the mission to southern Africa conducted by James Murray on the CG's behalf, focusing on South Africa, from the end of July to the end of August 1979. Within the framework of this overall unsuccessful mission, the proposal originally from Luanda for a demilitarised zone (DMZ) north and south of the Namibian border with Angola was revisited. A DMZ Conference was held under UN chairmanship in Geneva on 12-16 November 1979, attended inter alia by South Africa (accompanied by delegates of the internal parties), SWAPO, the FLS, Nigeria and the CG (as observers). However, the DMZ initiative failed to achieve its objective mainly due to conditions set by Pretoria.[99]

In February 1980, the SG dispatched General Prem Chand, who was due to assume command of UNTAG's military component, on an exploratory mission to Angola, Zambia, Botswana and Namibia. Subsequently, USG Brian Urquhard and the UNSR travelled to South Africa and the 5 FLS with the General on 4-14 March, also meeting SWAPO President Nujoma for talks in Luanda. Whilst the FLS and SWAPO obviously wished to launch SCR 435 quickly and largely accepted the delegation's proposals, no go-ahead could be obtained from Pretoria. In the further course of the year, South Africa posed individual questions on UNTAG and the super-

---

ance: DB 630 of 3.4.1979; DB 757 of 24.4.1979; DB 863 of 7.5.1979; DB 910 of 10.5.1979 – all from NY.

[99] For more on the Murray mission and the DMZ Conference: DB 1474 of 6.8.1979; DB 1562 of 16.8.1979; DB 1663 of 30.8.1979; DB 1684 of 31.8.1979; DB 1780 of 14.9.1979; DB 2771 of 8.11.1979; DB 3476 of 5.12.1979 – all from NY; SG report on the DMZ Conference of 20.11.1979 (S/13634) and 31.3.1980 (S/13862).

vision of SWAPO, but cited its general mistrust of UN "impartiality" as the main obstacle.

On 24 November 1980, in a bold attempt finally to create a break-through, the SG announced a "Pre-implementation Meeting" (PIM) for January 1981 as "a means of facilitating agreement and creating the necessary climate of confidence and understanding". Under UN chairmanship, the internal parties were also to be officially represented in addition to SWAPO and South Africa – a spectacular concession to Pretoria. The CG, the FLS, Nigeria and the OAU were to attend as observers. The main objective was to obtain a binding promise of a date for the ceasefire and thus the launch of the SCR 435 process, at the latest on 30 March 1981, so that the elections and subsequent independence could still be conducted in 1981.[100]

It was indeed a bold attempt, and the CG supported it loyally, but basically had no hope of overcoming the South African blockade. In particular, three topical factors suggested that South Africa was now less willing than ever to abandon its delaying tactics:

– First, the elections held in Rhodesia in February 1980 on the basis of the Lancaster House negotiations in London (Rhodesia gained independence as Zimbabwe on 18 April 1980) came as a shocking surprise to Pretoria. Robert Mugabe had emerged the clear winner, gaining an absolute majority with his ZANU party while the forces receiving intensive and diverse support from South Africa (in particular Bishop A. Muzorewa) only managed a pitiful 3% of the seats.[101] The impossibility of manipulating Black voters to any notable degree in free elections could not have been demonstrated more drastically.

---

[100] DB 863 of 31.3.1980 from NY; DB 122 of 12.5.1980 from Cape Town; letter from FM Botha to the SG of 12.5.1980 (S/13935); SG's letter to FM Botha of 20.6.1980 (S/14011); DB 1668 of 25.6.1980 from NY; SG's Report of 24.11.1980 (S/14266).

[101] Of the 100 seats in parliament, ZANU (Zimbabwe African National Union) won 57; ZAPU (Zimbabwe African People's Union), led by J. Nkomo and also fought by South Africa, won 20; the RF (Rhodesian Front), reserved for White settlers, won 20; and the forces supported by South Africa (A. Muzorewa) won 3 seats.

- Second, the DTA was rapidly losing ground in Namibia among the Black population. It had made impressive gains in the elections manipulated by South Africa in 1978 and dominated the building blocks of the "internal solution" ("Constituent Assembly", "National Assembly", "Council of Ministers"). But the DTA had lost half its supporters in 1980. In the event of an international settlement, Pretoria had always counted on being able to keep SWAPO in check with this party.
- Third, throughout 1980 the apartheid regime pinned its hopes on the election campaigns in the USA and in the Federal Republic of Germany. It felt there was a good chance of conservative forces gaining the upper hand there and finally liberating Southern Africa from President Jimmy Carter and FM Genscher, the CG's most energetic driving factors behind the UN settlement for Namibia. Although FM Genscher remained in office, the transfer of power in Washington to Ronald Reagan gave the Bothas such strong encouragement that the most obvious course of action for them in January 1981 was to sit back and wait for the new Republican Administration's policy on Africa to be announced.[102]

The PIM convened under the chairmanship of USG Urquhart in Geneva on 8-14 January 1981. For the first time in 66 years of de-facto colonial rule, South Africa sat down at the same table with a liberation movement. To the obvious satisfaction of Under-Secretary Fourie seated in the background (FM Botha did not put in an appearance), the representatives of the internal parties, in particular those from the DTA, took full advantage

---

[102] For more on the political constellation prior to the PIM and, in particular, on the three factors of South Africa's motivation dealt with here: DB 281 of 4.8.1980 from Pretoria; DB 1955 of 6.8.1980 from NY; DB 375 of 2.10.1980 from Pretoria; DE 5477 of 29.10.1980 from Section 320; DB 3075 of 29.10.1980 from NY; DB 3111 of 30.10.1980 from NY; DB 445 of 31.10.1980 from Pretoria; ministerial submission from Section 320 of 17.11.1980; DB 2263 of 17.11.1980 from Paris; ministerial submission from Section 320 of 26.11.1980.

of their speaking opportunity to raise their profile on the international stage, heaping attacks on SWAPO, some of which were abusive. SWAPO behaved quite differently. Much to the surprise of observers accustomed to the opposite, Nujoma remained patiently calm, assuring his willingness for a ceasefire and gaining recognition for his "statesman-like" conduct. On South Africa's behalf, AG Daniel Hough declared on 13 January that it was unreasonable to expect Pretoria and the internal parties to make the desired declaration of intent on a specific date because it had not been possible to overcome mistrust of the UN and SWAPO's intentions in the event of their election victory. On 14 January, Urquhard confirmed that the conference had failed and brought the PIM to a close without any specific proposals for the next steps.[103]

IV Deus ex machina

Leonhard Kremer, the German Ambassador in Dar es Salaam, who was always excellently informed and an objective analyst, reported on 23 January 1981 that Nyerere had stated internally among his advisers that, as SWAPO and the FLS had demonstrated their willingness to compromise in Geneva, Africa now had a right to call for the SC to impose sanctions under Article 41 of Chapter VII of the Charter. However, since a Western veto was to be expected, all that remained was intensified armed struggle with the aid of the Eastern Bloc. Kremer continued in his report that Nyerere, who was interested in stable relations with the CG states not least due to Tanzania's dependence on Western development aid, only wanted to raise the spectre of an escalating Communist role in order to persuade

---

[103] Course of the PIM Conference: DB 20 of 9.1.1981; DB 28 and 32 of 10.1.1981; DB 54 of 13.1.1981; DB 61 and 65 of 14.1.1981 – all from Geneva; *New York Times* of 14.1.1981; UN Press Release NAM/36 of 14.1.1981; DB 4 of 13.1.1981 from Cape Town; SWAPO spokesman Peter Nanyemba called the PIM "a pure waste of time". South Africa had exploited the Conference to "present its puppets". (DPA No. 197 of 26.1.1981).

the West finally to take tougher action against Pretoria. But the Tanzanian President saw the opposite coming: he feared that the Reagan Administration would make a direct connection between the Namibia issue and the Soviet-Cuban role in Angola, i.e. as a factor in the East-West power game and no longer primarily as an African concern worth supporting.[104]

As early as January 1981, the Federal Ministry of Foreign Affairs in Bonn also suspected that something sinister was looming from Washington. From the appearance of the new Secretary of State designate, General Alexander M. Haig, before the Senate Committee on 14 February, the German Embassy had learned that the candidate had avoided giving a clear answer to the question whether he supported SCR 435. London, Paris and Ottawa presumably also received corresponding messages.[105]

After uncertainty about the Reagan Administration's policy on Africa had dragged on until March 1981 and the resulting stagnation in Namibian affairs had further undermined the confidence of SWAPO, the FLS and all the African countries in the Western Five, FM Genscher wrote to FM Haig on 24 March demanding credible signals of Western movement before the new Administration announced its official line. Washington should dispatch a reputed US politician on a special stocktaking mission to the relevant African capitals. The five Foreign Ministers should then discuss the way forward in the margins of the Rome NATO Conference scheduled for May. FM Genscher knew that the British Foreign Secretary, Lord Carrington, and the Quai d'Orsay were also making similar approaches to Haig.[106]

In response, Haig announced that he would send the designated Assistant Secretary of State for African Affairs, Chester Crocker, on a special mission to Africa for consultations. Only then would the future US policy

---

[104]   DB 20 of 23.1.1981 from Dar es Salaam; DB 73 of 9.2.1981 from Addis Ababa.
[105]   DB 251 of 23.1.1981 from Washington; DB 129 of 23.1.1981 from NY.
[106]   Ministerial submission from Section 320 of 20.3.1981; DE of 18.3.1981 from Section 320 to UN New York; DB 1252 of 25.3.1981 from Washington.

on southern Africa be disclosed.[107] Crocker conducted the mission from 9 to 21 April 1981 and met leading Africa experts from the four other Foreign Ministries in London on 22 and 23 April for an initial evaluation.[108] It was clear at this meeting that Washington had already decided back in March 1981 to make Cuba's withdrawal from Angola a condition for US involvement in obtaining South African agreement to an internationally acceptable Namibia settlement. Without making the matter public, Haig hinted at this connection when he met his four counterparts in Rome on 3 May, then presented it frankly and in detail in Ottawa on 20/21 July. This US policy went down in the history of Namibian affairs under the designation "linkage". All four US partners immediately and clearly opposed the introduction of this condition in Ottawa, and none of their governments departed from this position at any later point.[109] They were fully in agreement with the assessment published later by ex-Secretary of State Vance:

> For the future, we should press ahead on the basis of Resolution 435 and the contact group plan. At the present stage of negotiations, it is self-defeating to seek to condition implementation of a settlement, as is being done, on Angola's commitment to terminate the Cuban presence prior to the departure of South African troops. The removal of Cuban forces will come in the natural course of events after South African withdrawal, but not before.[110]

Only the realisation that nothing could be achieved in southern Africa without the USA kept the Four from pulling out of the CG in open confrontation with the new US course. Outwardly, they did not deny the undoubted Western interest in Cuban withdrawal, but clearly stressed that

---

[107] DE from Section 320 to UN New York of 27.3.1981; DB 1335 of 30.3.1981 from Washington.
[108] DB 690 and 691 of 23.4.1981 from London.
[109] For more on the decision in March 1981 cf. Crocker loc.cit., pp.63-67; on the meeting in Ottawa on 20/21 July cf. Crocker loc.cit. pp.101-103.
[110] Author, ZEI loc.cit. pp.237/238; DB 129 of 23.1.1981 from NY; DB 18 of 26.1.1981 from Luanda; DB 33 of 8.2.1981 from Luanda.

they did not regard this as a package deal. The State Department occasionally tried to relativise the link by talking about "de-facto-parallelism" or "empirical simultaneity", claiming that there was an objective connection between the two problem scenarios but that they had to be tackled separately. Yet in talks with SG Waldheim on 13 April, FM Haig bluntly referred to "linkage", stating that the USA regarded the Namibia problem primarily from a global strategic point of view.[111] US circles around Crocker were overwhelmingly in favour of making a completely new start, and the Americans in the CG initially expressed contempt for the Namibia diplomacy to date; SCR 435 had failed and should be jettisoned.[112] In 1986, this evaluation still echoed in Crocker's own words at a hearing of the Senate Committee on Foreign Relations when he spoke of an "absence of a viable Western strategy for Namibia decolonisation" with reference to early 1981.[113] In actual fact, he had immediately seen the great value back in 1981 of the internationally recognised settlement plan negotiated with the conflicting parties. Crocker included SCR 435 fully in the further procedures, although he was keen to give the impression that the plan was unviable in its present form and required some creative redesigning to convert it into a realistic project: "constructive engagement". More on that subject in the next chapter. Despite differences of opinion, it has to be said that the other members of the CG regarded Chester Crocker as an educated and friendly colleague who was always prepared to listen.

"Linkage" exceeded South Africa's wildest hopes of what they could expect from the Reagan Administration. Except for the one single phase at the end of 1977, Pretoria had never again even hinted at a link between

---

[111] DB 1024 of 7.5.1981 from NY; DB 1911 of 12.5.1981 from Washington; DB 2007 of 16.5.1981 from Washington; Crocker loc.cit. p.122; for more on Haig's attitude cf. also Urquhart loc.cit. pp. 320/321.

[112] DB 1911 of 12.5.1981 from Washington.

[113] US Dptm. of State, Bureau of Public Affairs, Current Policy No. 796, published 18 February 1986.

Namibian independence and Cuban withdrawal. The apartheid regime had now finally been presented with a reliable barrier against SCR 435 and the pressure of UN sanctions since Brezhnev could be trusted: there was no fear of Moscow foregoing "its" Cuban presence in Southern Africa.[114]

V Two pillars of confidence: Constitutional Principles and "Impartiality Package"

The CG had insisted on its settlement proposal since 29 September 1978 (SCR 435) not only as a general foundation but also as specific rules for the political process of decolonising Namibia. It consistently resisted repeated attempts by the conflicting parties and forces in the Reagan Administration to re-negotiate parts of the proposal. At the same time, the CG was aware of two shortcomings in the framework conditions for the UN settlement from a very early stage:

First, statements by SWAPO had fuelled the mistrust, constantly fomented by Pretoria, among sections of the Namibian population who were against the liberation movement, with regard to the kind of Constitution to be expected in the event of a SWAPO victory. Of course, virtually all Whites harboured such fears.

Second, several GA Resolutions and UN practices which one-sidedly favoured SWAPO interests aroused the fear that UNTAG would not treat all parties fairly and equally during the transition process ("impartiality").

Not only did these elements of weakness in the basis of confidence frequently provide South Africa and the internal parties with credible fallback positions, eventually setting the tone for the PIM Conference. They also hampered all five CG governments in their efforts to persuade conservative

---

[114] DB 2456 of 18.6.1981 from Washington; ministerial submission from Section 320 (p.4) of 14.12.1981; DB 284 of 21.6.1981 from Pretoria. "Deus ex machina" (literally "God from the machine"): Theatrical device whereby a God is surprisingly lowered onto the stage by machinery and then averts a disaster.

critics at home. Tackling them openly before SCR 435was adopted would have had no prospect of success in view of SWAPO's radical support in the GA.

When they entered Namibian politics in spring 1981, Crocker and his assistants tried to create the impression that they had been the ones to discover these problem areas and had started to overcome them with "phase 1 and phase 2" of the new "constructive engagement". "Phase 3" was then supposed to obtain Pretoria's firm assurance of a definite date for the beginning of SCR 435 implementation. As the following shows, this was a highly subjective depiction of events which somewhat disconcerted the other four. The term "constructive hi-jacking" did the rounds.

It was back on 16 December 1979 that the author, in his capacity as the German CG representative at the Geneva DMZ Conference, submitted the proposal to establish binding regulations on the content of Namibia's future Constitution prior to the beginning of SCR 435 implementation in a report to the Foreign Ministry in Bonn, an English translation of which was circulated within the CG the same day. The proposal was modelled on the Lancaster House settlement for Rhodesia which was reached in London around that time. The report stated that the aim of these regulations was to dispel mistrust and fears about the future in South Africa and among the internal parties. As at Lancaster House, gaining the support of the FLS was a crucial factor here too. Instead of Great Britain and the USA in the case of Rhodesia, the CG was called upon to implement the initiative in the case of Namibia as the mediator with sufficient credibility.[115]

The idea of such confidence-building was raised several times within the CG in 1980.[116] In January 1981, before Crocker joined the CG (he

---

[115] DB 2055 of 16.11.1979 from Geneva; this report and its circulation in an English version is referred to in Weiland/Braham loc.cit. p.23 and in Engel/Schleicher loc.cit. pp.283/284.

[116] Ministerial submission from Section 320 of 31.7.1980; DB 1979 of 11.8.1980 from NY; DE of 13.8.1980 from Section 320 to Pretoria.

had started at the State Department at the beginning of 1981 but only received Senate confirmation of his official role on 9 June 1981), the Federal Ministry of Foreign Affairs had obtained a copy for the CG of a study entitled "Constitutional Options for Namibia" written by the Namibia Institute in Lusaka. In a letter to Secretary of State Haig on 24 March 1981, FM Genscher proposed "the binding agreement of important constitutional principles prior to implementation of the settlement plan" and mentioned that Paris also supported this idea.[117]

A CG meeting at the level of the five Africa Department heads was held in London on 22 and 23 April. Crocker represented the USA for the first time at this internal event. The Five decided to draft constitutional principles and to seek agreement on these principles in a negotiating process with South Africa and the internal parties, who were to be treated as full partners in this matter, as well as with the FLS and finally with SWAPO.[118]

On 21 July 1981, the five Foreign Ministers (Haig/USA, Genscher/Germany, Cheysson/France, Carrington/Great Britain, MacGuigan/Canada) decided in Ottawa that preparations for such negotiations should begin and, on the occasion of the opening session of the GA in New York on 24 September, approved the proposal which the CG had meanwhile drafted. This draft had been shaped by substantial German contributions and was consequently based to a large extent on Germany's Basic Law. After the relevant partners had been informed in advance about the draft, the CG undertook a diplomatic mission in an aircraft provided by Washington from 25 October to 6 November 1981, stopping off in Lagos, Lu-

---

[117] DB 15 of 26.1.1981 from Lusaka; ministerial submission from Section 320 of 20.3.1981; DB 1252 of 25.3.1981 from Washington.

[118] Ministerial submission from Section 320 of 21.4.1981; DB 690 of 23.4.1981 from London. From this date, CG meetings on important occasions were usually attended by the Africa Directors from the five Foreign Ministries. As a rule, Crocker as well as Robert Frasure and Mrs. Nancy Ely represented the USA, Wilhelm Haas, Ernst-Jörg von Studnitz and the author represented Germany, Jean Ausseil and Paul Dahan attended for France, Michael Shenstone and Eric Bergbush for Canada, and Leonhard Allinson and Mrs. Maeve Fort for Great Britain.

anda, Cape Town, Windhoek, Gabarone, Harare, Maputo, Lusaka, Dar es Salaam and Nairobi (since Kenya then chaired the OAU).[119]

The most difficult party to convince was obviously SWAPO rather than South Africa or Windhoek, and once again it was crucially important to obtain the support of the FLS and Nigeria. As expected, their consent could not be obtained straightaway.

Here too, it was especially important how President Nyerere (Tanzania), still FLS spokesman, reacted. He found the whole idea unhelpful. He had been waiting for success in vain for three years. SWAPO had confirmed its willingness to an immediate ceasefire at the PIM Conference. Where was the pressure on South Africa? Instead, these constitutional principles piled up new obstacles. One should leave the Constitution to the elected representatives. Yet despite all the frustration, it was clear that Nyerere saw no alternative to SCR 435 and thus to co-operation with the CG.

The reactions of the other Africans were not unfriendly, but also reserved. One exception came during the stopover in Harare on 31 October. It was the CG's first encounter with President Robert Mugabe. He listened calmly to the detailed explanations of the principles, then asked incisive questions, which revealed his full understanding and expertise in constitutional law. He presented a brilliant analysis of the problems still to be solved in southern Africa and promised to support the CG vis-à-vis SWAPO. Mugabe kept this promise. He carried conviction as a realistic and politically astute statesman. None of the CG delegates who witnessed him at that time could have imagined the extent of Zimbabwe's suffering under this man's irresponsible dictatorship 20 years later.

Nyerere organised a confidential meeting of the Foreign Ministers of the FLS and Nigeria with Nujoma in Dar es Salaam on 17 November

---

[119] For more on the preparations cf. DB 3887 and 3890 of 1.10.1981 from Washington. The CG delegates on this mission were: Crocker, Frasure (USA), Bergbush, Christopher Thomson (Canada), Allinson, Mrs. Maeve Fort (Great Britain), Paul Dahan (France), the author and Cornelius Sommer (Germany).

1981. After four hours of consultations, the local Ambassadors of the Five were handed a text representing the "final position of the FLS" on 18 November, which had been shortened and simplified in several places but was constructive overall. Unclear redrafting of passages on the principle of power sharing and the electoral system caused a problem. Out of consideration for the absence of clearly demarcated constituencies and the vital interests of the internal parties, the CG favoured a form of proportional representation, avoiding the Westminster system which was widespread in the region ("winner takes all"; the candidate attaining a majority in the constituency wins the seat, the other votes do not count). The CG initially tried in vain to introduce an electoral system along the lines of Germany's two-vote procedure. It subsequently took several *démarches* and contacts, especially on the electoral system, before the Five were finally in a position to report final agreement and present the constitutional principles, attached as Annex C (S/15287), on 12 July 1982.[120]

The document clearly states that a Constituent Assembly must first be elected according to democratic rules. With regard to the electoral system, the text is evasive: "The electoral system will seek to ensure fair representation in the Constituent Assembly to different political parties which gain substantial support in the election." This was followed by basic rights and suitable principles for the government and administration of a democratic state governed by the rule of law.

In fact, the constitutional principles were fully incorporated, without any inter-party dispute, into the Namibian Constitution drafted in Windhoek from 22 November 1989 to 9 February 1990.[121]

---

[120] For more on the CG meeting with Nyerere on 5.11.1981 cf. DB 479 of 7.11.1981 from Nairobi and DB 359 of 13.11.1981 from Luanda; on the FLS Conference of 17.11.1981 cf. DB 526 and 529 of 18.11.1981 from Dar es Salaam; on South Africa's statement cf. DB 4883 of 3.12.1981 from Washington; on the conclusion of negotiations on constitutional principles cf. DB 1713 of 12.7.1982 from NY; on Mugabe's role, which was still helpful later cf. DB 104 of 5.2.1989 from Harare.

[121] Paul Szasz in Weiland/Braham loc.cit. pp.243-256; DB 330 of 21.12.1989 from

In 1982, "impartiality" was a problem area which the New York CG had been tackling for quite some time. It was closely linked to the issue of the national origin of UNTAG personnel. As with the constitutional principles, SWAPO was also the conflict party primarily affected by "impartiality" and its consent had to be sought. Once again, everything depended on including the FLS in the diplomatic process. After the discussions in January 1979 mentioned above, the CG incorporated explicit reassurances in the guidelines for Murray's mission for a "fair and impartial electoral process" and "that the UNTAG military component will perform its duties capably and impartially". The SG received a letter from FM Botha on 12 May 1980 (S/13935) calling on the UN to abandon favouritism of SWAPO, especially in the following areas: application of the GA Resolutions on "sole and authentic representative", preferential treatment compared with other political parties in Namibia in UN bodies (observer status, right to speak), UN financial contributions. It was clear to everyone that a formal revocation of the designation "sole and authentic" was politically unachievable in the GA. However, the Five had always insisted that the SC was the prime decision-making body in the Namibia process and that it had never supported this designation. SG Waldheim referred to this priority competence of the Security Council in his letter of reply to FM Botha dated 20 June 1980 (S/14011). The CG drafted a detailed guarantee declaration by the SG, stating that the UN would meet Botha's other demands when the transition process began under SCR 435. The CG proposed confidential consultations on these sensitive issues initially with the FLS after SG approval. McHenry considered the idea of exchanging a confidential "package" of mutual declarations of intent (i.e. also from the South African side) for confidence-building in a "final phase".[122]

Windhoek.

[122] CG tabling of "impartiality" in January 1979, cf. footnote 93 above; guidelines for Murray's mission cf. DB 1291 of 3.7..1979 from NY; first CG "impartiality package" cf. DB 1391 of 29.5.1980; DB 1402 of 30.5.1980; DB 1532 of 11.6.1980, DB 2561

The CG discussed these guarantees with the FLS in the margins of the PIM conference in Geneva on 10 January 1981 and met with understanding. McHenry took this occasion to refer to the opinion expressed by Ben Gurirab (SWAPO) to the press that a SWAPO claim to sole representation would "no longer be necessary" once the transition process had actually started.[123]

In the light of these circumstances prior to the gradual familiarisation of new colleagues from the US Administration in spring 1981, it was astonishing to hear Chester Crocker claim that not only the constitutional principles but also the "impartiality package" had been American "fresh proposals" for entering with the CG into "restructured negotiation".[124]

When the CG conducted its above-mentioned mission to southern Africa in October/November 1981 they took with them discussion documents on "impartiality", which were based largely on preliminary work from 1980, but the negotiating situation was not conducive to the resolution of this difficult subject.[125] However, the CG subsequently rediscovered its traditional grand style of handling all manner of diplomatic dealings: by the end of July 1982, it had settled all the differences over "impartiality" and UNTAG. It met in New York, Washington and Ottawa. Progress was also frequently supported by the action of individuals coordinated with the CG and *démarches* made by the local Ambassadors in South Africa, the FLS and in dealing with SWAPO. Crocker predominantly represented the USA himself. As a result, the Africa Department heads from the other four capitals were also more directly involved than before.[126]

The principal objective with regard to South Africa was to obtain its promise to abolish the "National Assembly" and "Council of Ministers"

---

of 1.10.1980 – all from NY.

[123] DB 33 of 10.1.1981 from Geneva.

[124] Crocker loc.cit. pp.101/102 and pp.119-123.

[125] DB 2173 and 2174 of 6.10.1981; DB 2211 and 2212 of 8.10.1981; DB 2332 of 15.10.1981 – all from NY; DE from Section 320 to UN New York, i.a. of 12.11.1981.

[126] Main CG protagonists as in footnotes 118 and 119 above.

in Windhoek as well as demobilisation of the South West African Territorial Force (SWATF, about 10,000 men) established through compulsory military service imposed by Pretoria. The South Africans were gradually persuaded by the Americans. These were preliminary stages of an "internal solution" which were clearly incompatible with SCR 435, which South Africa had accepted, and thus in breach of international law. All expert observers were unanimously convinced that Washington could also have obtained the necessary South African measures, which were easy for Pretoria to take, without "linkage" if they had been prepared to send appropriate signals of pressure. It was not about such petty details, but about a clear South African commitment to a date for implementing SCR 435; Crocker had nothing to contribute to this ("phase 3"). The only outstanding issue regarding UNTAG was composition of the military component. Pretoria did not oppose the participation of contingents from non-aligned states or even Eastern Europe (Romania), requesting only that no blue helmets should be considered from countries which South Africa regarded as allied with SWAPO, e.g., Ghana, Nigeria, Panama, Bangladesh, India and Yugoslavia. There were even misgivings about the Finns (already too numerous in Namibia, in particular missionaries in Ovamboland), which made Ahtisaari prick up his ears. It finally proved possible to placate South Africa with the assurance that the SG would not proceed with the composition of UNTAG against a South African veto. In fact, with the exception of Nigeria and Ghana, South Africa did not later oppose the participation of these countries.[127]

As indicated above, the Five faced the much more difficult task of persuading SWAPO, with help from the FLS, to meet Botha's demands in the above-mentioned letter to the SG of 12 May 1980. Through multilateral consultations the CG slowly but surely drafted a list of "impartiality" concerns with the aim of reaching a confidential agreement. The CG was

---

[127] DB 2483 of 2.6.1982 from Washington; DB 2301 of 24.5.1982 from Washington.

well aware that it was not realistic to expect SWAPO to make an official declaration of renunciation in a UN document. At the same time, it placed a large number of South African obligations at the top of the list – a superfluous gesture since Pretoria had already accepted them under SCR 435 – in order to create the semblance of a balanced compromise package (cf. Annex D).

Things came to a head at the Canadian UN Mission in New York within the framework of the CG consultation round with the FLS, Nigeria, Kenya and SWAPO on 6-9 July 1982. The declared objective – also shared by Crocker – was to reach agreement on all unresolved issues so as to enable the SC to take a decision at the end of July on the start of SCR 435 implementation in order to commence actual implementation of this Resolution in late August/ early September.

The African side entered the round with a distinct willingness to reach a rapid understanding with the CG. The process of seeking agreement benefited hugely from the participation of three extremely competent FLS representatives who argued calmly and objectively: Paul Rupia (UN Ambassador from Tanzania), Joseph Legwaila (UN Ambassador from Botswana) and Fernando Honwana (Mozambique). It was thus possible to discuss important issues and declare them unanimously resolved without written notes. The issues clarified in advance with South Africa included e.g. the scope of the UNSR's supervisory functions; UNTAG supervision of SWAPO in Angola and Zambia with the co-operation of UN liaison offices; equal status of the former police and the South West Africa Police Force (SWAPF) established by South Africa after SCR 435; and the delicate question of how to deal with armed SWAPO fighters present in Namibia prior to the ceasefire. Everyone had to bear in mind that South African resistance to the new establishment of a SWAPO camp was insurmountable and that there was also a serious risk of armed SWAPO groups there being challenged and killed by the South African armed forces. The call for such a camp was dropped, which could only be

91

seen as SWAPO's willingness to hand weapons brought into the country over to UNTAG.

On the basis of the above-mentioned "informal check list" (Annex D) drafted by the CG, agreement was reached on the cessation of all UN payments to SWAPO and its renunciation of preferential treatment in UN bodies, details of UN supervision of the police, the monitored demobilisation of SWATF and SC competence to decide the composition of UNTAG on the basis of GA proposals discussed with the parties involved.

At the final meeting on 9 July, Germany assumed the rotating chair of the CG and the author (then Head of Section 320 at the Foreign Ministry) became the chairman. The essential movements towards an agreement were achieved at this meeting. The chairman subsequently reported the following to his Minister:

> After the Africans had departed, the Five looked at one another incredulously. Progress seemed almost too great and too fast. If the outcome of 9 July holds, we can assume that the African side is determined to take the Five at their word with their timetable and deny SWAPO virtually all opportunities to apply the brakes.[128]

The list was treated as a confidential "non-paper" and called an "impartiality package". Those involved regarded the contents as a binding confidential agreement. Consequently, it was not published in 1982 (at the request of the African side). Only SG Pérez de Cuéllar was notified in advance by the Head of Section 320 on 26 July and then jointly by representatives of all the parties involved on 24 September 1982. On behalf of the Five, a CG mission led by the author informed the internal parties about the cur-

---

[128] For more on the course of this round: DB 1665 of 6.7.1982; DB 1675 and 1678 of 7.7.1982; DB 1687 of 8.7.1982; DB 1702 and 1703 of 9.7.1982 –all from NY; UNTAG supervision of SWAPO camps in Angola and Zambia was later confirmed in the SG Report of 19.5.1983 (S/15776) and in SCR 532 of 31.5.1983.

rent state of affairs in Windhoek on 30/31 July. This completed the CG's work on the two confidence-building flanks of SCR 435.[129]

From this moment on, Pretoria raised no further credible objections to the peaceful settlement. If this had been President Reagan's goal, he would undoubtedly have possessed sufficient internal political backing at the end of 1982 to enforce SCR 435 against opposition from South Africa. Individually, the other four would hardly have been in a position to act against the one-sided interests of their respective business lobbies, i.e. robustly threaten sanctions, but they would certainly have been willing and able to follow a resolute US leadership.

---

[129] DB 1780 of 26.7.1982 from NY; author in ZEI loc.cit., p.237; on the CG mission to Windhoek DB 1781 of 26.7.1982 from NY; Section 320's submission to Under-Secretary of 2.8.1982; New York Times of 1.8.1982 "Namibian Accord is Expected Soon."

C 1982 to 1990: A crisis-ridden process of perseverance with a happy ending

I   Insistence on SCR 435 despite the "linkage"

In 1981/82, the Cuban issue was a largely suppressed topic both within the CG and among the African countries, hidden behind the veils of Crocker's "Phase One and Phase Two", held firmly in place by the State Department. Now the veils had floated away and instead of the "phase three" diva dressed in her finery, namely Pretoria's agreement to the commencement of UNTAG, it was "linkage" that stood alone on the stage, naked and ugly.

The Americans had fostered the impression that Cuban withdrawal was within reach. Crocker had openly supported and even encouraged CG expectations that the SC would adopt the Resolution to commence SCR 435 implementation before the end of 1982 and that Namibian independence could thus be achieved in 1983. Secretary of State George P. Shultz, Haig's successor since June 1982, had also publicly announced together with the four other Foreign Ministers in New York on 1 October that the Foreign Ministers welcomed "the constructive and flexible attitude of the parties" and that "a valuable opportunity now existed to achieve a settlement in the time-frame envisaged".[130]

In reality, such expectations were in no way borne out by the true state of American-Soviet relations and Washington's contacts with Luanda. At the meeting of the Five in Paris on 8 August 1982, Crocker had been forced to admit that two missions by US General Vernon Walters to Luanda had been unsuccessful. Angola strictly rejected "parallelism" and even

---

[130] For a revealing insight into the Five's embarrassment: DB 2282 of 1.10.1982 from NY; DB 1450 and 1451 of 5.8.1982 from Paris.

abandoned the original offer to initiate Cuban withdrawal following Namibia's declaration of independence. It now insisted instead that this independence first had to be convincingly consolidated. The German side suggested that, rather than the American "linkage", South Africa could be offered an Angolan guarantee supported by the FLS that Cuban withdrawal would be conducted after independence. The Americans dismissed this suggestion.[131]

The machinations and tugs-of-war staged by Washington outside the CG in the period that followed were not a decisive factor in Namibia's liberation and do not merit a detailed account here. One thing is certain: the "linkage" policy did not achieve its objective in what were six bitter years for Namibia. According to a statement by Crocker to the House of Representatives Sub-Committee on Africa on 15 February 1983, there were 20,000 to 25,000 Cuban soldiers in Angola at the time. In 1988 the figure was 50,000. What was then finally initiated in 1988 (on the basis of the New York Agreements of 22 December between Angola and Cuba as well as between South Africa, Angola and Cuba) would also have occurred without "linkage" due to the change in Soviet UN and security policy prepared by Mikhail Gorbachev from 1985 and openly propagated and vigorously practised world-wide from 1988.[132] Cuban auxiliary forces gradually

---

[131] Meeting of the Five in Paris on 8.8.1982: Crocker/Frasure, Ausseil/Gueguinou/Dahan, Squire (Great Britain), Lapointe, Head of Section 320. DB 1450 of 5.8.1982 from Paris.

[132] When the two agreements (S/20345 and S/20346) were ceremonially signed by FM Botha, FM van Dunem (Angola) and FM Malmierca (Cuba) in the presence of SG Pérez de Cuéllar and Secretary of State Shultz in the large ECOSOC conference room at the UN East River headquarters on 22.12.1988, James Murray, the Deputy Head of the French UN Mission and the author were also present. The CG was not given a single mention in the speeches by the SG and the four Ministers praising the negotiating process (cf. DB 3451 and 3452 of 23.12.1988 from New York). After the US "success" of the "linkage" drama, Angola remained in misery and civil war for over a decade. For more on the presentation of the US approach by Chester Crocker, "High Noon in Southern Africa", New York 1992, cf. critical account in: Seiler, J., "Destructive Engagement", in Weekly Mail of 24.6.1993; Brittain, V., review

disappeared from the whole of Africa. On the other hand, without Crocker's input – or one might rather say, despite the Reagan Administration – Pretoria's resistance was virtually exhausted in 1988. PM Botha's propaganda about the threat of a "total communist onslaught" from neighbouring states and inside the country from ANC now just seemed ridiculous. The political opposition within South Africa, full of self-confidence and ready to fight, was becoming ever more difficult to control and took increasing encouragement from the growing resonance of international anti-apartheid movements, particularly in Europe. South Africa no longer had military superiority in southern Angolan airspace. The crisis-torn economy was rattled by the increase in voluntary sanctions imposed by the West. In Namibia, the political party DTA was weakened to such a large extent that Pretoria could not abide by its plan to build an "internal solution" chiefly on the DTA or to deploy the DTA as a viable opponent to SWAPO in international elections.

These prospects could not be anticipated in 1983. The CG was taken by the words of its Foreign Ministers of 1 October 1982 and came under increasing fire at the UN. The fact that rapid progress towards a peaceful transition process was blocked for the time being by US policy prompted some authors to conclude that the CG had suspended its activities; that it had failed. As later evidence will show, this was a misjudgement which can only be explained by the limited access to authentic information, especially written source material.[133]

---

in The Guardian, London, of 25.5.1993; Vale, P., "Crocker's Choice", in The South African Journal of International Affairs, Vol.1, No.1, 1993; Davidson, B., "Bloody-Minded", in London Review of Books, 9.9.1993, pp. 13/14. On general criticism of "linkage", cf. Kühne, W., "Frieden im Südwestlichen Afrika?", in Europa Archiv, 44th edition, no. 4 of 25.2.1989, p. 108; FM Ben Gurirab (Namibia) 1992 in Weiland loc. cit., p.47. On Crocker's appearance before the Sub-committee in 1983, cf. DB 727 of 16.2.1983 from Washington.

[133] Stating the end of the CG's activities: Claudius Wenzel: "Südafrika-Politik der Bundesrepublik Deutschland 1982 bis 1992", DUV 1994, p. 119; Brenke loc.cit., p. 264; Engel-Schleicher loc.cit. p. 294; Henning Melber: "Die Dekolonisation Namibias", in

Apart from the particularly intensive consultations undertaken by the Five in the years 1983/84, which are recounted in detail below, the following can be said in general about CG continuity: Despite the "linkage", which was already in the air at the time, the Five achieved two of their most important negotiating successes in efficient group action with Crocker's participation in 1982. Consequently, "linkage" cannot be held responsible for causing CG stagnation. But the group also subsequently remained on standby year after year. Those wiser after the event fail to appreciate that back in 1982 there was no sign of a gaping void stretching ahead to 1988. No one, not even Crocker himself, expected such a protracted delay, each maintaining the hope nurtured by Washington and their own contacts that the process would start the following year at the latest. It was therefore a case of conducting constant activity to sustain the level of consensus with the FLS and SWAPO as far as possible and prevent them abandoning the advanced stage of agreement already reached. But it cannot be denied that the issues which made for exciting direct negotiations with the conflicting parties to shape the settlement plan had now been resolved, and the CG was less in the limelight as a result. In fact, from 1986 there were almost three years of virtually paralysing demoralisation due to the evident US military support for the Angolan rebel movement UNITA, after the US Congress had rescinded the 1976 Clark Amendment (no military aid to any party in Angola) on 10 July 1985. Given such a contradictory constellation, how was the indispensable agreement with the MPLA government in Luanda supposed to be reached in the foreseeable future?[134]

Jahrbuch Dritte Welt 1990, published by Deutsches Übersee-Institut Hamburg, pp. 203-223; Jabri loc.cit., p. 110. Such assumptions already appear in the CHRISTIAN SCIENCE MONITOR of 2.6.1981: "Black Africa angry at Reagan offer of trade off to Pretoria." Example of CG consultation in 1986, cf. DB 790 of 16.4.1986 (Ahtisaari talks to the CG in New York on 14 April about his visits to Luanda and Lusaka).

[134] Author in ZEI loc.cit. pp.237-239; for more on the Clark Amendment cf. Jabri loc. cit. p.162; and on the US debate about tougher sanctions on South Africa, cf. Crocker loc.cit., pp.264-267.

At continued CG meetings held at local working level in New York in 1983/84 and – at the persistent initiative of the Head of Section 320 - also in Bonn, but above all in consultations by the five Foreign Ministers and the five Africa Directors, it was repeatedly made clear that the USA was responsible for solving the problem arising from "linkage" and that this was not part of the CG's programme. At the same time, these meetings were of course dominated by the interest of the Four in reliable information on the current state of affairs and by their concern to maintain the CG's indispensable credibility vis-à-vis the FLS and SWAPO. They left no one in any doubt that they were waiting urgently for any kind of success or a change in the Reagan policy and were naturally also prepared themselves – outside the CG's Namibia Initiative – to offer possible assistance with regard to Cuban withdrawal, which was a general wish of the Western countries. The CG co-ordinated its appearance at the SC and GA, analysed the internal situation in South Africa and Namibia and exchanged information gained from bilateral contacts with the African side.

At FM Genscher's suggestion, the five Foreign Ministers met for consultations on the occasion of the World Economic Summit in Williamsburg/USA on 28/29 May 1983. Secretary of State Shultz hosted a dinner which was attended by FM Cheysson, FM Genscher, FM Allen MacEachen(Canada) and Under-Secretary Bullard (Great Britain). Genscher stated at this gathering that, from Moscow's point of view, "linkage" promoted the South Africans to "useful idiots". Further talks on Namibia at FM level were held in Paris on 8 June 1983. Directors' meetings attended by Crocker were held inter alia: in 1983, on 24/25 February in Ottawa, on 15/16 May in Bonn; in 1984, on 6 February in London, on 3 May and 14 November in Bonn; in 1985, on 16 July in London.

Publicly, Paris was particularly opposed to linking Reagan's policy on Angola with the SCR 435 issues. There were already signs of this in France's contribution to the general debate at the 37th GA in New York on 30 September 1982. After FM Cheysson had also emphasised this divergence in the French National Assembly (7 December 1983), he made it clear to the four CG colleagues in the margins of the Brussels NATO conference in December 1983 that France saw no further point in collaborating in the CG as long as Washington's insistence on "linkage" blocked the path to a Namibia settlement. Although France's Africa Director Jean Ausseil still participated in the CG meetings in Bonn on 14 November 1984 and London on 16 July 1985, subsequent CG meetings were held for a long time without any French representative.

Some have interpreted this as French abandonment of the CG and thus as proof of its failure. Paris has never officially confirmed that. France refused to go along with the growing impression among its African partners and the UN that it would be roped into an unaccepted US project. However, France never cast doubt on its solidarity with the original CG initiative or its willingness to support implementation of SCR 435. Correspondingly, the French always kept themselves fully informed via working level contacts. It was more a temporary "empty chair" policy. This unilateral action was of course regretted by the other Four and perceived at the UN as an additional burden on CG credibility. As we shall see later, France fully collaborated again in the CG's efforts to remove doubts about the "impartiality package" in New York in 1989 once the issue of "linkage" had been resolved.[135]

II SWAPO and German Namibians get to know one other

In addition to activities within the CG framework, each of the five governments contributed towards promoting the UN settlement for Namibia.

---

[135] Brenke loc.cit, p.101; Engel/Schleicher loc.cit. p.294; Jabri loc.cit. p.108 and pp.155-161 (also more details there on the background); letter of 2.2.1984 from FM Genscher to FM Cheysson cf. telegraphic instruction from Section 320 to Paris, e.g. of 6.2.1984; on France's participation in the CG meeting in 1985 cf. ministerial submission from Section 320 of 22.7.1985.

Special traditional links (Great Britain) as well as the extent and content of various economic relations (Great Britain, USA, France and Germany) played a role vis-à-vis South Africa, whereas with the FLS it was primarily post-colonial ties and diverse forms of development aid.

In the case of the Federal Republic of Germany it was naturally assumed that, as a result of the German Empire's colonial rule which ended in 1915 and the existence of about 23,000 Namibians of German descent (of whom about 6,400 were citizens of the Federal Republic of Germany) at the time of the Five's initiative, the German government would be under specific pressure to act in the Namibia issue. These circumstances did indeed provide considerable material for discussion in the fierce dispute between the political parties in the Federal Republic of Germany where government policy on southern Africa was at times bitterly opposed by the CDU/CSU, and the Bavarian CSU chairman Franz-Joseph Strauß in particular repeatedly carried the debate to polemical extremes. But although the interests of German Namibians had always been important to FM Genscher, who had been able to determine policy on Namibia constantly until 1990, he would nevertheless have been just as intensely committed to the UN settlement even without this factor. As well as avoiding SC sanctions against South Africa, he was primarily interested in ensuring that the central concern of German CSCE policy and *Ostpolitik*, namely to demand human rights and the right to self-determination, was given international visibility. At the same time, he was keen for the Federal Republic of Germany, which was a relatively new member of the UN (1973) and a first-time member of the Security Council in 1977/78, to present a convincing profile – particularly to the Third World. For Genscher, the SCR 435 settlement was also a preliminary step towards overcoming apartheid in South Africa and thus a contribution towards reducing the vociferous criticism of Germany's relations with this country.[136]

---

[136] Author in ZEI loc.cit. pp.224-227; author in *Zeitschrift für die UN* 2002, volume 2, pp.48/49; for more on the polemics of Franz-Joseph Strauß, cf. e.g., *Der Spiegel,*

Despite vehement opposition at home, FM Genscher consistently stuck to his conviction in his assessment of the liberation movements in southern Africa that these movements were fighting for national independence and the right of self-determination; that their susceptibility to problematical Eastern Bloc interference was a consequence of the failure of the West, which had left them in the lurch in their legitimate struggle; and that this did not justify their indiscriminate categorisation as Communists and terrorist gangs subservient to Moscow. From the very beginning, the German side thus contributed within the CG to accepting SWAPO as a partner. Genscher had an initial meeting with Nujoma in the margins of the New York proximity talks on 12 February 1978. This was followed by a second encounter in September, once again in New York, at which the SWAPO leader made a remarkable suggestion: the Foreign Minister should encourage the German Namibians to stay; they were Namibians and did not need to fear expropriation without compensation. Genscher invited Nujoma to Bonn. After a further exchange of ideas in Salisbury on 23 April 1980, Nujoma visited Bonn on 22-24 October and stayed at the official guesthouse of the Federal Ministry of Foreign Affairs. The SWAPO leader developed a trusting relationship with Genscher which over the years made the German Foreign Minister his preferred contact within the Five and manifestly reinforced Germany's role in the CG. There were further visits to Bonn in May 1981 and June 1982. The first encounter between Crocker and Nujoma was arranged in the margins of the latter visit. At the end of 1982, SWAPO established a Representation in Bonn with the Federal Republic's approval and financed by the Friedrich Ebert Foundation. Opposing German forces attempted to prevent Nujoma from returning to the German capital in 1984. The Munich branch of the *Deutsch-Südafrikanische Gesellschaft* filed charges against Nujoma with the Public Prosecutor's office for alleged murder and participation in offences involving explosives. Gen-

No. 32, p.28, of 4.8.1986.

scher pre-empted any possible difficulties by inviting the SWAPO partner, who was in Paris at the time, to the splendid Palais Beauharnais (German Ambassador's residence) on 18 February 1984, without mentioning the politically absurd campaign against him. Further contacts followed. For their last encounter prior to independence, the SWAPO leader came to Bonn for extensive talks with FM Genscher and Minister of State Helmut Schaefer (Federal Ministry of Foreign Affairs) on 2-5 March 1989, during which a secret meeting with South Africa's Ambassador to Bonn (Retief) was arranged.[137]

Thanks to its special relations with SWAPO, Germany was able to make a contribution, which was highly acknowledged by all the CG partners, to undemonising the liberation movement and removing the deep-seated mistrust which virtually all Whites in Namibia felt towards it. In 1977, a group of German Namibians in Windhoek led by Konrad Lilienthal formed the *Interessengemeinschaft Deutscher Südwester (IG)* (Community of Interests of German-speaking South-Westers). Initially just a few hundred strong, the group grew to 2,200 members by 1987. To begin with, this association had openly supported the DTA. Later, however, it increasingly adopted a realistic position based on SCR 435, which was not shared by the majority of rather conservative German Namibians who rejected a UN-brokered settlement.

In July 1980, the IG approached the German Embassy in Pretoria and asked the Federal Government to set up an initial, confidential meeting with SWAPO. Genscher subsequently arranged for Under-Secretary Günther van Well to invite the IG board members Lilienthal, Staby, Weitzel and

---

[137] For more on Genscher's SWAPO diplomacy cf. author in ZEI loc.cit. pp.235/236; analysis of SWAPO by Karl Flittner, Under-Secretary's submission from Section 320 of 13.12.1982; Nujoma's visit to Bonn in May 1981: DE from Section 320 to Maputo, i.a. of 29.5.1981; Nujoma's visit to Bonn in March 1989: DE from Section 320 to NY, i.a. of 14.3.1989. For more on the Nujoma-Crocker encounter in Bonn: ministerial submission from Section 320 of 24.5.1982 and DB 2517 of 3.6.1982 from Washington.

H. Schneider to a dinner at the residence of the German UN Ambassador in Geneva with Nujoma, Ben Gurirab and Hamutenya of SWAPO in the margins of the PIM Conference on 9 January 1981. The IG and SWAPO spent over three hours alone together after the dinner. To the surprise of the IG representatives, the SWAPO leader was engaging and unpolemical. They were amazed at the extent to which their own ideas tallied with those of Nujoma, who expressed his basic commitment to the rule of law and constructive cooperation with Whites. His movement had learned its lessons from the devastating consequences of the Portuguese exodus from Angola and Mozambique. – As expected, the IG's advance, considered sensational and scandalous at home, triggered aggressive mistrust especially in South Africa and among the DTA, which was vented in accusations of "opportunist treachery", "alliance with terrorists" and a "separate deal in favour of the German Namibians" at Bonn's instigation.[138]

Further rounds of IG-SWAPO talks, mediated and financed by Bonn, took place i.a. in Paris (1982), Harare (1983), Lusaka (1984) and Harare (1987), enabling them to deal objectively with one another and develop an understanding of common interests and objectives. On the German side, Africa Director Wilhelm Haas and from 1984 his successor Hans Günter Sulimma rendered outstanding services on behalf of these projects. The IG was not afraid of revealing its contacts in Windhoek, thus becoming a multiplier for the view among a considerable number of Whites that it would be possible to live with SWAPO.[139] The CG was kept constantly informed of all these events.

---

[138] DB 263 of 23.7.1980 from Pretoria; DB 29 and 30 of 10.1.1981 from Geneva; DB 16 of 27.1.1981 from Cape Town; DB 30 of 6.2.1981 from Cape Town; DB 44 of 23.2.1981 from Cape Town.

[139] Author in ZEI loc.cit. p.236; for more about Konrad Lilienthal cf. Wilhelm Haas "Gästebücher", MediaPuzzle, Berlin 2002, pp.119-128.

III Late rebellion against the basis of confidence

In the days following the New York agreements of 22 December 1988, the SC began consultations on the Resolution now needed to authorise the launch of UNTAG. African delegates, supported by Brazil, surprised everyone by claiming that the "impartiality package" of July 1982 had been merely an informal arrangement and was not legally binding on the GA, the SC or other parties not directly involved. Evidently, these delegates had been insufficiently informed about the events of 1982. As a result, the very basis of the deal was at risk of being undermined, which was particularly unacceptable for South Africa.

At the suggestion of the author, who was Deputy Head of the German UN Mission at the time, the New York CG immediately convened for a meeting in his office in December 1988. A representative of the French UN Mission also came to this meeting. The CG agreed that everyone should immediately seek clarifying talks in the UN with representatives of SWAPO, the FLS and Nigeria known to them and hand over a copy of the "impartiality package". At the same time, *démarches* by the local Five were undertaken as a group or individually in the FLS capitals. SG Pérez de Cuéllar also recognised the danger. In his report of 23 January 1989 (S/20412), he explicitly stressed in items 35 and 36 that this agreement formed part of the binding principles of the settlement plan. In order to put an end to the uncertainties still circulating in the Africa Group, he then officially published the "impartiality package" as an SC and GA document at Germany's suggestion on 16 May 1989 (S/20635 and A/44/280).

Nevertheless, the attacks assumed increasingly ominous forms. The elections in Namibia were meanwhile scheduled for 7 to 12 November 1989. In early October, a group from the Council for Namibia was still campaigning openly against any binding effect of the 1982 agreements beyond the elections. Only those elected would subsequently have a say and the GA would then also no longer be prevented from debating the Namibia issue anew. It was thus clear that even the constitutional principles were being questioned. The group was evidently toying with the plan that, in the event of an unsatisfactory outcome to the elections, it would not only contest the results with the help of the great majority of non-aligned states in the GA but would also send the entire SCR 435 process back to the drawing board. At the same time, forces within the Council for Namibia were intent on divesting the AG of his powers if the elections went in their favour and entrusting the Council for Namibia with Namibia's administration. This was a blatant infringement of the operative paragraph 1 of SCR 435 in conjunction with the SG's report S/12827 of 29 August 1978 (item 14). The spokesmen for this disruptive group was the chairman of the Council for Namibia, UN Ambassador Peter D. Zuze (Zambia), UN Ambassador Mudenge (Zimbabwe) and – surprisingly – UN Ambassador Paulo Nogueira-Batista (Brazil). The CG had the impression that these protagonists were acting mainly without specific instructions from their capitals. Such independent characters, frequently encountered at the UN, were referred to in the CG as "unguided missiles".

The CG in New York had to contend with this alarming affront even after the elections. The author always took the initiative, and meetings were held in his UN Mission. Bob Rosenstock and Terry Jennings attended on behalf of the USA, Stewart Eldon for Great Britain, Mrs. Gail Miller, Mrs. Lillian Thomsen and Philippe Kirsch for Canada. Pierre Menat, the designated French representative, only took part occasionally and indirectly; his instructions seemed to be unclear. In agreement with the capitals, the CG now intensified the above-mentioned campaign of contact and *démarches* with more extensive documentation. SWAPO had not been among the instigators of the attempted sabotage and relented after the elections. The crisis was finally averted.[140]

---

[140] Germany was a non-permanent SC member for the second time in 1987/88. DB 3490, 3491 and 3494 of 31.12.1988 from NY; DB 1325 of 25.7.1989 from NY; for more on the crisis of Oct/Nov 1989: GA Document A/44/597 of 2.10.1989;

IV Time lost in the Security Council with serious consequences

By adopting SCR 629 on 16 January 1989, the SC decided that 1 April 1989 should be the date on which implementation of SCR 435 would begin, that the SG should arrange a formal ceasefire with South Africa and SWAPO for that date and prepare at the earliest possible date a report to the SC on the planned implementation of UNTAG.

The SG presented this report on 23 January (S/20412). The five permanent SC members had previously insisted that the costs for UNTAG were to be kept within limits and that cost-saving criteria should be applied when planning the number of UNTAG personnel in particular. Basing his report on a budget of US$ 416 million, the SG proposed in item 54g an initial figure of only 4,650 out of the originally planned 7,500 blue helmets. This led to an unprecedented confrontation between the permanent five and the non-aligned who were not prepared to accept that additional troop requirements would have to be approved by the SC, which meant that they could be blocked by a veto. Agreement was eventually reached on a supplementary declaration by the SG enabling him to state that the SC had assured him of their prompt and "fullest co-operation" in the event of additional requirements (S/20457). This budget-related dispute caused weeks of delay to UNTAG's deployment in Namibia in preparation for 1 April, which was to prove partly responsible for the tragic events to be dealt with later.[141]

At noon on 16 February 1989, the SC finally took the unanimous decision to begin implementation of SCR 435 by adopting SCR 632. In an

---

DB 2018 and 2019 of 20.10.1989 from NY; DB 2044 of 20.10.1989 from London; DB 2202 of 31.10.1989 from NY; DB 2398 of 7.11.1989 from NY; DB 2643 of 20.11.1989 from NY.

[141] For more on the background to the delay: DB 61 of 16.1.1989; DB 131 of 30.1.1989; DB 170 of 2.2.1989; DB 216 of 10.2.1989 – all from NY; on the authorising Resolution SCR 632 of 16.2.1989 cf DB of 16.2.1989 from NY to Section 230 (File Ref.: Pol 381.42 NAM); on GA approval of the UNTAG budget cf. DB 343 of 1.3.1989 from NY.

outburst of joy unprecedented in the SC, all the members jumped to their feet and applauded. From the observer seats, 435-veteran James Murray shouted across to the author with a laugh that he had a framed copy of SCR 435, signed by all five CG Foreign Ministers who were in office in 1978, hanging in his living room.

The GA did not approve the budget until 1 March 1989.

V SWAPO throws a spanner into the works

From late March/ early April 1989 there were no longer any South African armed forces in Angola. Consequently, SWAPO was bound by the terms of Article 5 of the Geneva Protocol of 5 August 1988, to which Nujoma had agreed, namely that all SWAPO combat troops in Angola had to be deployed to the north of the 16th parallel (over 120 km north of the Namibian border).[142] On 14 March 1989, the SG suggested to South Africa and SWAPO that the ceasefire should commence at 4 a.m. Greenwich Mean Time (6 a.m. in Namibia) on 1 April. Nujoma and FM Botha agreed to this proposal in writing on 18 and 21 March 1989 respectively. In his letter, Nujoma once again confirmed "… SWAPO's acceptance of the de facto cessation of armed hostilities in and around Namibia between South Africa and SWAPO, in accordance with the Geneva Protocol of 5 August 1988."

On 1 April 1989, the joyful celebrations in Windhoek and elsewhere in Namibia to mark the onset of change were interrupted by news that armed SWAPO units were crossing the border from Angola and were engaged in bloody fighting with the police in Ovamboland. FM Botha, who was in Windhoek that day, accused UNTAG of failure and threatened to

---

[142] The Geneva Protocol is an agreement between Angola, South Africa and Cuba. Nujoma agreed to its terms in a letter dated 12.8.1988 (S/20129); cf also on this whole topic the SG's Report of 23.1.1989 (S/20412) and South Africa's letter to the SG of 4.4.1989 (S/20565 and S/20566).

abandon the SCR 435 process. But PM Margaret Thatcher, who happened to be passing through Windhoek on the way to visit the Roessing Mine near Swakopmund (owned by the British-Canadian Rio Tinto Company), made a more judicious statement around midnight, declaring that she was in favour of convening an immediate meeting of the SC, that she would meet Mikhail Gorbachev next week and wished to discuss the situation with him. In response to Botha's threat that South Africa would send its troops back in, Thatcher replied that UNTAG now had military control over Namibia and that it was solely UNTAG's task to manage the crisis.

Unfortunately, this was precisely the problem. It became increasingly apparent that over 1,000 heavily armed SWAPO fighters had gradually appeared in northern Namibia. Due to the drastic delay in approval of the UN budget, there had not been sufficient time for the UNSR to deploy the UNTAG personnel envisaged for the border region and southern Angola. Observers reported that, according to reliable sources, there were no more than 9 (nine) members of UNTAG in the northern region concerned on 1 April. Ahtisaari immediately sent 4 UN staff on a recce visit to the North. The official UN report reads as follows:

> The team of UNTAG officials sent to the North held discussions on 2 April with South African security forces and interviewed two SWAPO prisoners captured the previous day. The latter said that they had been instructed by their commanders in Angola to enter Namibia, avoiding South African security forces if possible, in order to establish bases in Namibia under United Nations supervision. Their units were to bring with them all their arms, including rockets and anti-aircraft devices.
>
> ... the captives, who had impressed the UNTAG team with their credibility ...

The Embassy of the Federal Republic of Germany in Luanda reported on 3 April that the Angolan authorities also seemed to assume that the SWAPO fighters came from Angola. In addition, several missionary reports had confirmed that SWAPO units were still in the southern part of Cunene

Province. On 2 April, Ahtisaari decided that limited units of the regular South African forces should deploy from their supervised bases to assist the over-burdened police in the task of detaining SWAPO fighters. He had previously agreed the following with the SG:

> Certain specific units, to be agreed, will be released from restriction to base to provide such support as may be needed by the existing police forces, in case they cannot handle the situation by themselves. The situation will be kept under constant review and the movement out of existing bases will throughout be monitored by UNTAG military observers.

Considering that the UNTAG deployment was incomplete, the second sentence contained a lot of wishful thinking. The South African military dealt with the situation in their own way. Sustaining 32 casualties among their own army and police force, they killed about 300 SWAPO fighters and captured others. The UN strongly condemned this brutal excess. But the UN themselves faced criticism from various quarters for the delay in deployment: although the UNTAG mandate did not provide for violent intervention, the critics rightly assumed that the lethal use of weapons would have been kept within limits if blue helmets had been present in sufficient numbers. At the same time, it must be said that Ahtisaari never intended to grant the South African forces scope for such violence and that he saved the SCR 435 process with his courageous decision which was not without personal risk.

On 8 April, the SWAPO leadership gave the order for their fighters to cease hostilities, regroup and deploy back to Angola under UNTAG supervision within 72 hours. The following day, a commission established in December 1988 and consisting of representatives from Angola, SA and Cuba (with observers from the USA and the Soviet Union) issued the Mount Etjo Declaration, calling on all SWAPO combatants to make their way to designated assembly points, hand their weapons over to UNTAG and be repatriated to Angola under UNTAG supervision. The Angolan representatives evidently also assumed that SWAPO insurgents had crossed the border into Namibia. In view of the violent actions of their adversaries, who included members of the feared special para-military unit *Koevoet* (crowbar) re-activated by South Africa, and the weak UNTAG presence, virtually no one went to the assembly points. Instead, the SWAPO fighters crossed the border independently with their weapons, which resulted in further casualties. South Africa paid no heed to the urgent appeals from both the SG and the Commission to avoid violence. It was not until 19 May that all SWAPO military forces were finally reported to be north of the 16th parallel and all South African armed forces at UNTAG-monitored bases in Namibia. The situation called for on 1 April had been achieved at last. The UN report stated: "It had been a nightmare beginning to an operation which had been launched with so much hope.[143]

What induced SWAPO to make this mistake? It is still not clear whether Nujoma personally sanctioned the disastrous orders. To this day, SWAPO maintains that its fighters were already in Namibia prior to the ceasefire. There is no denying that the largely SWAPO-loyal Ovambo population might well have secretly harboured large numbers of fighters before 1 April. However, considering the dense police infiltration of even Ovamboland, it seems unlikely that over 1,000 such uniformed combatants, some of whom were bearing heavy arms which would have been difficult to conceal, could have been there on 31 March ready to be deployed. But even if one presumes this version is true, the order to emerge into the open was irresponsible. SWAPO had been informed by its UN representation about the UNTAG delay. It was also obvious to its omnipresent sympathisers in Ovamboland that the blue helmets were absent and assembly points

---

[143] For more on the April crisis cf. United Nations, The Blue Helmets loc.cit. pp. 216-219; Weiland/Braham loc.cit. pp. 73-88; DB 39 of 2.4.1989 from Windhoek; DB 154 of 3.4.1989 from Luanda; DB 40 of 3.4.1989 from Windhoek; DB 597 of 5.4.1989 from NY; 2 South African letters to the SG of 4.4.1989 (S/20565 and S/20566); non-aligned movement communication to the SG of 6.4.1989 (S/20595); Mount Etjo Declaration S/20579; continuation of fighting, cf. DB 68 of 19.4.1989 from Windhoek; end of the crisis, cf. DB 94 of 20.5.1989 from Windhoek.

had not been prepared. The fighters could not possibly have expected the police to remain passive observers during the hours around the ceasefire. SWAPO accepted the risk of bloody fighting through the violent opposition of its combatants and thus a breach of the ceasefire.

The initiators certainly did not plan any large-scale armed confrontation. It is more likely that they intended to use the time remaining before the ceasefire began to reappear unscathed in their own country, hand themselves over to UNTAG there and have the constantly desired bases established. This is how they wanted to demonstrate their heroic success as Namibia's military liberators in the election campaign. The statement in the Waldheim Report of 26 February 1978 (S/13120) that SWAPO fighters in Namibia at the time of the ceasefire were to be confined to bases within Namibia, probably contributed to building the semblance of legitimisation, even though this passage was controversial from the very beginning and had long since been overtaken by later agreements. Pretoria had explicitly rejected this report. For South Africa, the well-known fact that SWAPO had never established fixed bases in Namibia and should not now be allowed to obtain them surreptitiously at the last moment was an absolutely indispensable condition for participating in the settlement process. Independent of South African propaganda, there are clear indications that at least some SWAPO fighters infiltrated after the ceasefire began, thus breaking the clear promise to remain north of the 16th parallel.

VI Then silence fell

From then on, UNTAG was able to carry out its mandate, although it had various difficulties to overcome.[144] 4,493 UN military personnel and about 3,500 UN civilian staff (of which 1,500 for police duties) were deployed

---

[144] Enlightening on UNTAG implementation: SG's reports of 6.10.1989 (S/20883), 3.11.1989 (S/20943), 14.11.1989 (S/20967), 29.11.1989 (S/20967/Add.1); SCR 643 of 31.10.1989; Notes of SC President of 20.11.1989 (S/20974).

in total. 97% of registered voters took part in the elections held from 7 to 11 November 1989. Only 1.4% of the ballots cast were declared invalid. 670,830 Namibians had cast valid votes. There were to be 72 seats in the Constituent Assembly.

According to SC Document S/20967, page 10, the election results were as follows:

SWAPO:	57.3% =	41 seats
Democratic Turnhalle Alliance:	28.5% =	21 seats
United Democratic Front:	5.6% =	4 seats
Action Christian National:	3.5% =	3 seats
Federal Convention of Namibia:	1.6% =	1 seat
National Patriotic Front:	1.6% =	1 seat
Namibia National Front:	0.8% =	1 seat

This Assembly adopted the Namibian Constitution by consensus on 9 February 1990. Independence was to follow on 21 March.[145]

The sport stadium in Windhoek was completely overcrowded that day. There was an almost suffocating crush of people blocking the entrance to the separate large VIP stand. FM Genscher, who was also hemmed in, held his arms out protectively around his wife to shield her from the crowd. Together with Egyptian President Mubarak they were pushed forward inch by inch. It was Genscher's 63rd birthday. In the end, they all found a seat. The opening of the independence celebrations had been delayed by over an hour.

Then silence fell.

After festive speeches, the South African flag was lowered and the Namibian flag hoisted. To the sounds of military music, a final unit of the former police marched in orderly fashion out of the stadium and SWAPO

---

[145] DB 50 of 12.2.1990 from Windhoek; DB 91 of 18.5.1990 from Windhoek.

soldiers entered. People felt that this marked the beginning of a way out of apartheid for the whole of southern Africa. Beside Nujoma stood the South African Prime Minister Frederik Willem de Klerk and Nelson Mandela - two great statesmen. Night had fallen, fireworks lit up the sky and the people in the stadium started to sing.

The whole country was at peace.

Bibliography

This account of events is based largely on "reporting telegrams" (DB) available to the author. These are telexes sent by German missions abroad to the Federal Ministry of Foreign Affairs reporting officially relevant information gathered by German diplomats abroad. The author himself wrote a considerable number of the reporting telegrams quoted as source material.

Ansprenger, Franz, Die SWAPO. Profil einer Afrikanischen Befreiungsbewegung. Munich, 1984

Bley, Helmut, Der Kampf um die koloniale Sozialordnung in Deutsch-Südwestafrika 1894-1914. Hamburg, 1968

Brenke, Gabriele, Die Bundesrepublik Deutschland und der Namibia-Konflikt. Munich (Oldenbourg), 1989

Crocker, Chester A., High Noon in Southern Africa. New York (Norton), 1992

Cubitt, Gerald (and Richter), Südwest. Cape Town (Struik), 3rd edition 1979

Diescho, Joseph, The Namibian Constitution in Perspective. Windhoek (Namibia Institute for Democracy), 1994

Engel/Schleicher, Engel, Ulf (and Schleicher), Die beiden deutschen Staaten in Afrika. Hamburg (Institut für Afrika-Kunde), 1998

Franck, Thomas M., Fairness in International Law and Institutions. Oxford (Clarendon Press), 1995

Franck, Thomas M., Recourse to Force. Cambridge (Cambridge University Press), 2002

Haas, Wilhelm, Gästebücher. Berlin, 2002

Hampson, Fen Osler, Nurturing Peace: Why Peace Settlements Succeed or Fail. Washington D.C. (United States Institute of Peace Press), 1996

Jabri, Vivienne, Mediating Conflict. Decision-making and Western Intervention in Namibia. Manchester and New York (Manchester University Press), 1990

Jaenecke, Heinrich, Die weißen Herren. 300 Jahre Krieg und Gewalt in Südafrika. Ed. Henri Nannen. Hamburg (Verlag Gruner und Jahr),1976, p. 189 ff.

Klein, Eckart, Namibia. In: Encyclopedia of Public International Law, vol. 3, Amsterdaym (Elsevier), 1997

Kühne, Winrich, Südafrika und seine Nachbarn: Durchbruch zum Frieden? Baden-Baden, 1985

Kunig, Philip, Das völkerrechtliche Prinzip der Nichteinmischung. Zur Praxis der OAU und des afrikanischen Staatenverkehrs. Baden-Baden (Nomos-Verlag), 1981

Melber, Henning, Conflict Mediation in the Process of Decolonisation: Resolution 435(1978) and Namibia's Transition to Independence. Centre for Conflict Resolution.

Melber, Henning, Die Dekolonisation Namibias. In: Jahrbuch Dritte Welt 1990, Hamburg (Deutsches Übersee-Institut), pp. 203-223

Murray, Roger et al., The Role of Foreign Firms in Namibia. Uppsala, 1974

Nachtwei, Winfried, Namibia. Von der antikolonialen Revolte zum nationalen Befreiungskampf. Mannheim, 2nd ed., 1976

Steltzer, Hans Georg, Die Deutschen und ihr Kolonialreich. Frankfurt (Societäts-Verlag), 1984

United Nations, The Blue Helmets. A Review of United Nations Peacekeeping. New York (UN Department of Public Information), 3rd ed., New York, 1996

Urquhart, Brian, A Life in Peace and War. New York (Harper & Row), 1987

Vance, Cyrus, Hard Choices. New York (Simon & Schuster), 1983

Vergau, Hans-Joachim, Namibia-Kontaktgruppe: Katalysator des Interessenausgleichs. In: Zeitschrift für die VN, 50, 2, 2002, pp.48-50

Vergau, Hans-Joachim, ZEI, Genscher und das südliche Afrika. In: Schriften des Zentrums für Europäische Integrationsforschung, vol 50 (Genscher, Deutschland und Europa), Baden-Baden (Nomos-Verlag), 2002, pp..223-239

Verheugen, Günter, Apartheid, Südafrika und die deutschen Interessen am Kap. Cologne, 1986

Weiland/Braham, Weiland, Herbert (and Braham) (eds.)., The Namibian
  Peace Process: Implications and Lessons for the Future. Freiburg i.B.
  (Arnold Bergstraesser Institut), 1994. Including the contributions by
  *Don McHenry, p 13 ff. Hans-Joachim Vergau, p. 18 ff. Martti Ahtisaari,
  p. 59 ff. Prem Chand, p. 89 ff. Paul Szasz, p. 141 and p. 241 ff.*
Wenzel, Claudius, Südafrika-Politik der Bundesrepublik Deutschland
  1982-1992. Wiesbaden (Deutscher Universitäts-Verlag), 1994

Annexes

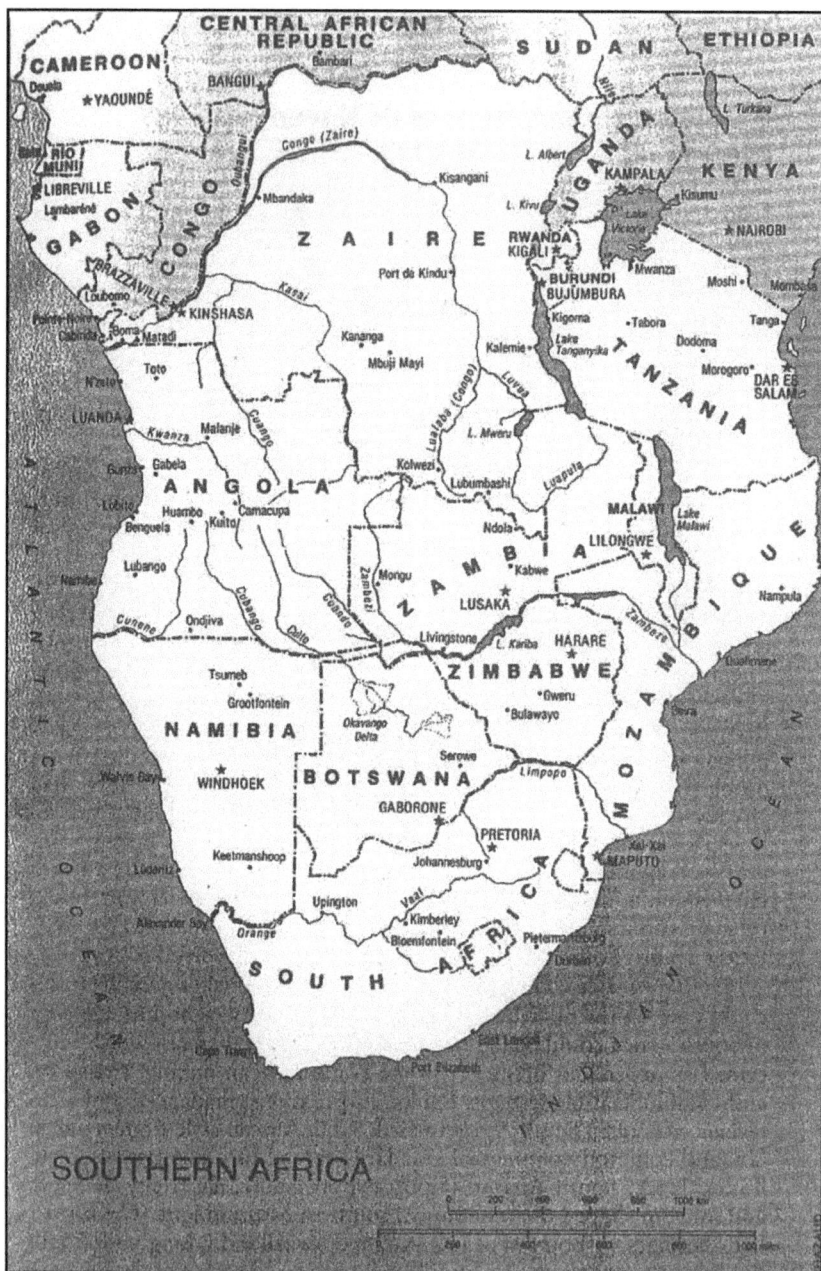

SOUTHERN AFRICA

UNTAG military deployment as of November 1989

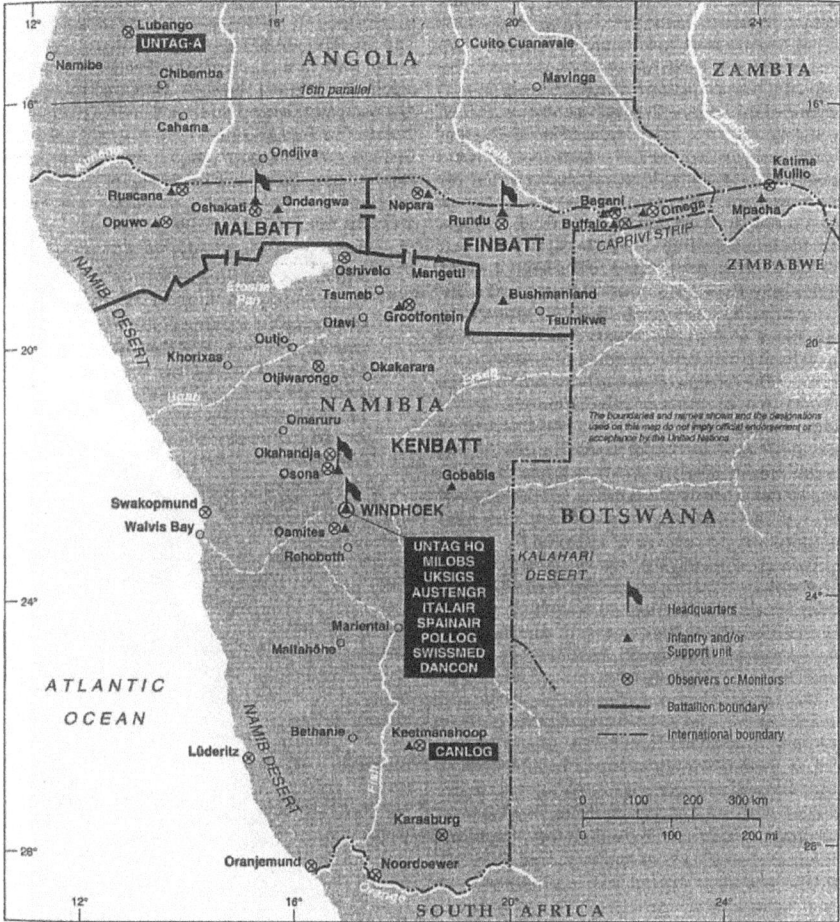

ANGOLA

ZAMBIA

Lubango
UNTAG-A
Namibe
Chibemba
16th parallel
Mavinga
Cuito Cuanavale

Cahama

Ondjiva
Katima
Mulilo

Ruacana
Oshakati
Ondangwa
Nepara
Begani
Omega
Mpacha
Opuwo
MALBATT
Rundu
Buffalo
CAPRIVI STRIP

FINBATT
ZIMBABWE

Oshivelo
Mangetti
Taumeb
Grootfontein
Bushmanland
Etosha Pan
Otavi
Tsumkwe

Outjo
Khorixas
Okakarara
Otjiwarongo

NAMIBIA

Omaruru

Okahandja
KENBATT
Osona
Gobabis

Swakopmund
WINDHOEK
BOTSWANA

Walvis Bay
Oamites
KALAHARI
DESERT

Rehoboth
UNTAG HQ
MILOBS
UKSIGS
AUSTENGR
ITALAIR
SPAINAIR
POLLOG
SWISSMED
DANCON

Mariental
Headquarters

Maltahöhe
Infantry and/or
Support unit

ATLANTIC
OCEAN
Observers or Monitors

Battalion boundary

Bethanie
International boundary

Lüderitz
Keetmanshoop
CANLOG

0   100   200   300 km
0   100   200 mi

Karasburg

Oranjemund
Noordoewer
SOUTH AFRICA

The boundaries and names shown and the designations used on this map do not imply official endorsement or acceptance by the United Nations

NAMIB DESERT

Map No. 3952.14   UNITED NATIONS
September 1996

Department of Public Information
Cartographic Section

119

Annex A

UNITED NATIONS

SECURITY

COUNCIL

Distr.
GENERAL

S/12636
10 April 1978

ORIGINAL: ENGLISH

LETTER DATED 10 APRIL 1978 FROM THE REPRESENTATIVES OF CANADA, FRANCE, GERMANY, FEDERAL REPUBLIC OF, THE UNITED KINGDOM OF GREAT BRITAIN AND NORTHERN IRELAND AND UNITED STATES OF AMERICA ADDRESSED TO THE PRESIDENT OF THE SECURITY COUNCIL

On instructions from our Governments we have the honour to transmit to you a proposal for the settlement of the Namibian situation and to request that it be circulated as a document of the Security Council.

The objective of our proposal is the independence of Namibia in accordance with resolution 385 (1976), adopted unanimously by the Security Council on 30 January 1976. We are continuing to work towards the implementation of the proposal.

(Signed) William H. BARTON
Permanent Representative of Canada
to the United Nations

M. Jacques LEPRETTE
Permanent Representative of France
to the United Nations

Rüdiger von WECHMAR
Permanent Representative of the
Federal Republic of Germany to
the United Nations

James MURRAY
Deputy Permanent Representative of the
United Kingdom of Great Britain and
Northern Ireland to the United Nations,
Chargé d'Affaires, a.i.

Andrew YOUNG
Permanent Representative of the
United States of America to the
United Nations

78-07488   /...

120

Annex A

S/12636
English
Page 2

<u>Proposal for a settlement of the Namibian situation</u>

I. Introduction

1.   Bearing in mind their responsibilities as members of the Security Council of
the United Nations, the Governments of Canada, France, the Federal Republic of
Germany, the United Kingdom and the United States have consulted with the various
parties involved with the Namibian situation with a view to encouraging agreement
on the transfer of authority in Namibia to an independent government in accordance
with resolution 385 (1976), adopted unanimously by the Security Council on
30 January 1976.

2.   To this end, our Governments have drawn up a proposal for the settlement of
the Namibian question designed to bring about a transition to independence during
1978 within a framework acceptable to the people of Namibia and thus to the
international community. While the proposal addresses itself to all elements of
resolution 385 (1976), the key to an internationally acceptable transition to
independence is free elections for the whole of Namibia as one political entity
with an appropriate United Nations role in accordance with resolution 385 (1976).
A resolution will be required in the Security Council requesting the Secretary-
General to appoint a United Nations Special Representative whose central task will
be to make sure that conditions are established which will allow free and fair
elections and an impartial electoral process. The Special Representative will be
assisted by a United Nations Transition Assistance Group.

3.   The purpose of the electoral process is to elect representatives to a Namibian
Constituent Assembly which will draw up and adopt the Constitution for an
independent and sovereign Namibia. Authority would then be assumed during 1978
by the Government of Namibia.

4.   A more detailed description of the proposal is contained below. Our
Governments believe that this proposal provides an effective basis for implementing
resolution 385 (1976) while taking adequate account of the interests of all
parties involved. In carrying out his responsibilities the Special Representative
will work together with the official appointed by South Africa (the Administrator-
General) to ensure the orderly transition to independence. This working
arrangement shall in no way constitute recognition of the legality of the South
African presence in and administration of Namibia

II. The electoral process

5.   In accordance with Security Council resolution 385 (1976), free elections will
be held, for the whole of Namibia as one political entity, to enable the people of
Namibia to freely and fairly determine their own future. The elections will be
under the supervision and control of the United Nations in that, as a condition to
the conduct of the electoral process, the elections themselves, and the
certification of their results, the United Nations Special Representative will
have to satisfy himself at each stage as to the fairness and appropriateness of

/...

Annex A

S/12636
English
Page 3

all measures affecting the political process at all levels of administration
before such measures take effect. Moreover the Special Representative may himself
make proposals in regard to any aspect of the political process. He will have at
his disposal a substantial civilian section of the United Nations Transition
Assistance Group, sufficient to carry out his duties satisfactorily. He will
report to the Secretary-General of the United Nations, keeping him informed and
making such recommendations as he considers necessary with respect to the
discharge of his responsibilities. The Secretary-General, in accordance with the
mandate entrusted to him by the Security Council, will keep the Council informed.

6.   Elections will be held to select a Constituent Assembly which will adopt a
Constitution for an independent Namibia. The Constitution will determine the
organization and powers of all levels of government. Every adult Namibian will
be eligible, without discrimination or fear of intimidation from any source, to
vote, campaign and stand for election to the Constituent Assembly. Voting will be
by secret ballot, with provisions made for those who cannot read or write. The
date for the beginning of the electoral campaign, the date of elections, the
electoral system, the preparation of voters rolls, and other aspects of electoral
procedures will be promptly decided upon so as to give all political parties and
interested persons, without regard to their political views, a full and fair
opportunity to organize and participate in the electoral process. Full freedom of
speech, assembly, movement and press shall be guaranteed. The official electoral
campaign shall commence only after the United Nations Special Representative has
satisfied himself as to the fairness and appropriateness of the electoral
procedures. The implementation of the electoral process, including the proper
registration of voters and the proper and timely tabulation and publication of
voting results will also have to be conducted to the satisfaction of the Special
Representative.

7.   The following requirements will be fulfilled to the satisfaction of the
United Nations Special Representative in order to meet the objective of free and
fair elections:

A.   Prior to the beginning of the electoral campaign, the Administrator
General will repeal all remaining discriminatory or restrictive laws, regulations,
or administrative measures which might abridge or inhibit that objective.

B.   The Administrator General shall make arrangements for the release, prior
to the beginning of the electoral campaign, of all Namibian political prisoners
or political detainees held by the South African authorities so that they can
participate fully and freely in that process, without risk of arrest, detention,
intimidation or imprisonment. Any disputes concerning the release of political
prisoners or political detainees shall be resolved to the satisfaction of the
Special Representative acting on the independent advice of a jurist of
international standing who shall be designated by the Secretary-General to be
legal adviser to the Special Representative.

C.   All Namibian refugees or Namibians detained or otherwise outside the
territory of Namibia will be permitted to return peacefully and participate fully
and freely in the electoral process without risk of arrest, detention,
intimidation or imprisonment. Suitable entry points will be designated for these
purposes.

/...

122

Annex A

S/12636
English
Page 4

D. The Special Representative with the assistance of the United Nations High Commissioner for Refugees and other appropriate international bodies will ensure that Namibians remaining outside of Namibia are given a free and voluntary choice whether to return. Provision will be made to attest to the voluntary nature of decisions made by Namibians who elect not to return to Namibia.

8. A comprehensive cessation of all hostile acts shall be observed by all parties in order to ensure that the electoral process will be free from interference and intimidation. The annex describes provisions for the implementation of the cessation of all hostile acts, military arrangements concerning the United Nations Transition Assistance Group, the withdrawal of South African forces, and arrangements with respect to other organized forces in Namibia, and with respect to the forces of SWAPO. These provisions call for:

A. A cessation of all hostile acts by all parties and the restriction of South African and SWAPO armed forces to base.

B. Thereafter a phased withdrawal from Namibia of all but 1500 South African troops within 12 weeks and prior to the official start of the political campaign. The remaining South African force would be restricted to Grootfontein or Oshivello or both and would be withdrawn after the certification of the election.

C. The demobilization of the citizen forces, commandos, and ethnic forces, and the dismantling of their command structures.

D. Provision will be made for SWAPO personnel outside of the territory to return peacefully to Namibia through designated entry points to participate freely in the political process.

E. A military section of the United Nations Transition Assistance Group to make sure that the provisions of the agreed solution will be observed by all parties. In establishing the military section of UNTAG, the Secretary-General will keep in mind functional and logistical requirements. The Five Governments, as members of the Security Council, will support the Secretary-General's judgement in his discharge of this responsibility. The Secretary-General will, in the normal manner, include in his consultations all those concerned with the implementation of the agreement. The Special Representative will be required to satisfy himself as to the implementation of all these arrangements and will keep the Secretary-General informed of developments in this regard.

9. Primary responsibility for maintaining law and order in Namibia during the transition period shall rest with the existing police forces. The Administrator General to the satisfaction of the United Nations Special Representative shall ensure the good conduct of the police forces and shall take the necessary action to ensure their suitability for continued employment during the transition period. The Special Representative shall make arrangements when appropriate for United Nations personnel to accompany the police forces in the discharge of their duties. The police forces would be limited to the carrying of small arms in the normal performance of their duties.

/...

Annex A

S/12636
English
Page 5

10. The United Nations Special Representative will take steps to guarantee against the possibility of intimidation or interference with the electoral process from whatever quarter.

11. Immediately after the certification of election results, the Constituent Assembly will meet to draw up and adopt a Constitution for an independent Namibia. It will conclude its work as soon as possible so as to permit whatever additional steps may be necessary prior to the installation of an independent Government of Namibia during 1978.

12. Neighbouring countries shall be requested to ensure to the best of their abilities that the provisions of the transitional arrangements, and the outcome of the election, are respected. They shall also be requested to afford the necessary facilities to the United Nations Special Representative and all United Nations personnel to carry out their assigned functions and to facilitate such measures as may be desirable for ensuring tranquillity in the border areas.

Annex A

S/12636
English
Annex
Page 1

ANNEX

Timing	SAG	SWAPO	UN	Other action
(1) At date unspecified:			UNSC passes resolution authorizing SYG to appoint UNSR and requesting him to submit plan for UN involvement. SYG appoints UNSR and dispatches UN contingency planning group to Namibia. SYG begins consultations with potential participants in UNTAG.	
(2) As soon as possible, preferably within one week of Security Council action:			SYG reports back to UNSC. UNSC passes further resolution adopting plan for UN involvement. Provision is made for financing.	
(3) Transitional period formally begins on date of UNSC passage of resolution adopting SYG's plan:	General cessation of hostile acts comes under UN supervision. Restriction to base of all South African forces including ethnic forces.	General cessation of hostile acts comes under UN supervision. Restriction to base.	As soon as possible: UNSR and staff (UNTAG) arrive in Namibia to assume duties. UN military personnel commence monitoring of cessation of hostile acts and commence monitoring of both South African and SWAPO troop restrictions. Begin infiltration prevention and border surveillance. Begin monitoring of police forces. Begin	Release of political prisoners/detainees wherever held begins and is to be completed as soon as possible.

AG = Administrator General; SAG = South African Government; SWAPO = South West Africa People's Organisation
SYG = Secretary-General of the United Nations; UN = United Nations; UNSR = United Nations Special Representative;
UNSC = United Nations Security Council; UNTAG = United Nations Transition Assistance Group

/...

Annex A

ANNEX (continued)

Timing	SAG	SWAPO	UN	Other action
			monitoring of citizen forces, ethnic forces, and military personnel performing civilian functions. UNSR makes necessary arrangements for co-ordination with neighbouring countries concerning the provisions of the transitional arrangements.	Establishment in Namibia of provisions to facilitate return of exiles. Establishment and publication of general rules for elections.
(4) Within six weeks:	Restriction to base continues. Force levels reduced to 12,000 men.	Restriction to base continues.	Appropriate action by UN High Commissioner for Refugees outside Namibia to assist in return of exiles. All UN activity continues.	Completion of repeal of discriminatory laws and restrictive legislation. Dismantlement of command structures of citizen forces, commandos and ethnic forces, including the withdrawal of all South African soldiers attached to these units. All arms, military equipment, and ammunition of citizen forces and commandos confined

/...

126

Annex A

ANNEX (continued)

Timing	SAG	SWAPO	UN	Other action
				to drill halls under UN supervision. AG to ensure that none of these forces will drill or constitute an organised force during the transitional period except under order of the AG with the concurrence of UNSR. AG with concurrence of UNSR determines what circumstances whether and under those military personnel performing civilian functions will continue those functions.
(5) Within nine weeks:	Restriction to base continues. Force levels reduced to 8,000 men.	Restriction to base continues. Peaceful repatriation under UN supervision starts for return through designated entry points.	All UN activity continues.	Completion of release of political prisoners/detainees wherever held.
(6) Within 12 weeks:	Force levels reduced to 1,500 men, restricted to Grootfontein or Oshivelo or both. All military installations along northern border would by now either be deactivated or put under civilian control under UN supervision.	Restriction to base continues.	All UN activity continues. Military Section of UNTAG at maximum deployment.	

/...

127

Annex A

English
Annex
Page 4

ANNEX (continued)

Timing	SAG	SWAPO	UN	Other action
	Facilities which depend on them (e.g., hospitals, power stations) would be protected where necessary by the UN.			
(7) Start of thirteenth week:				Official start of election campaign of about four months' duration.
(8) On date established by AG to satisfaction of UNSR:				Election to Constituent Assembly.
(9) One week after date of certification of election:	Completion of withdrawal.	Closure of all bases.		Convening of Constituent Assembly.
(10) At date unspecified:				Conclusion of Constituent Assembly and whatever additional steps may be necessary prior to installation of new government.
(11) By 31 December 1978 at latest:				Independence.

128

Annex B

UNITED NATIONS
SECURITY
COUNCIL

Distr.
GENERAL

S/RES/435 (1978)
29 September 1978

RESOLUTION 435 (1978)

Adopted by the Security Council at its 2087th meeting
on 29 September 1978

The Security Council,

Recalling its resolutions 385 (1976) and 431 (1978), and 432 (1978),

Having considered the report submitted by the Secretary-General pursuant to paragraph 2 of resolution 431 (1978) (S/12827) and his explanatory statement made in the Security Council on 29 September 1978 (S/12869),

Taking note of the relevant communications from the Government of South Africa addressed to the Secretary-General,

Taking note also of the letter dated 8 September 1978 from the President of the South West Africa People's Organization (SWAPO) addressed to the Secretary-General (S/12841),

Reaffirming the legal responsibility of the United Nations over Namibia,

1.   Approves the report of the Secretary-General (S/12827) for the implementation of the proposal for a settlement of the Namibian situation (S/12636) and his explanatory statement (S/12869),

2.   Reiterates that its objective is the withdrawal of South Africa's illegal administration of Namibia and the transfer of power to the people of Namibia with the assistance of the United Nations in accordance with resolution 385 (1976);

3.   Decides to establish under its authority a United Nations Transitional Assistance Group (UNTAG) in accordance with the above-mentioned report of the Secretary-General for a period of up to 12 months in order to assist his Special Representative to carry out the mandate conferred upon him by paragraph 1 of Security Council resolution 431 (1978), namely, to ensure the early independence of Namibia through free and fair elections under the supervision and control of the United Nations·

78-21191

/...

Annex B

S/RES/435 (1978)
English
Page 2

4.   <u>Welcomes</u> SWAPO's preparedness to co-operate in the implementation of the Secretary-General's report, including its expressed readiness to sign and observe the cease-fire provisions as manifested in the letter from the President of SWAPO dated 8 September 1978 (S/12841);

5.   <u>Calls on</u> South Africa forthwith to co-operate with the Secretary-General in the implementation of this resolution;

6.   <u>Declares</u> that all unilateral measures taken by the illegal administration in Namibia in relation to the electoral process, including unilateral registration of voters, or transfer of power, in contravention of Security Council resolutions 385 (1976), 431 (1978) and this resolution are null and void;

7.   <u>Requests</u> the Secretary-General to report to the Security Council no later than 23 October 1978 on the implementation of this resolution.

Annex C

**UNITED
NATIONS**

S

Security Council

Distr.
GENERAL

S/15287
12 July 1982

ORIGINAL: ENGLISH

LETTER DATED 12 JULY 1982 FROM THE REPRESENTATIVES
OF CANADA, FRANCE, GERMANY, FEDERAL REPUBLIC OF,
THE UNITED KINGDOM OF GREAT BRITAIN AND NORTHERN
IRELAND AND THE UNITED STATES OF AMERICA ADDRESSED
TO THE SECRETARY-GENERAL

On instructions from our Governments we have the honour to transmit to you the text of Principles concerning the Constituent Assembly and the Constitution for an independent Namibia put forward by our Governments to the parties concerned in the negotiations for the implementation of the proposal for a settlement of the Namibian situation (S/12636) in accordance with Security Council resolution 435 (1978) adopted on 29 September 1978.

We have pleasure in informing you that all parties to the negotiation now accept these Principles. Our Governments believe that a decision on the method to be employed to elect the Constituent Assembly should be made in accordance with the provision of Security Council resolution 435 (1978). All parties are agreed that this issue must be settled in accordance with the terms of Security Council resolution 435 (1978) and that the issue must not cause delay in the implementation of 435 (1978). In this regard, our Governments are in consultation with all parties.

131

Annex C

S/15287
English
Page 2

We have the honour to request that this letter and the Principles be
circulated as a document of the Security Council.

(Signed) Gérard PELLETIER
Permanent Representative of Canada
to the United Nations

(Signed) Luc de La BARRE de NANTEUIL
Permanent Representative of France
to the United Nations

(Signed) Ernst-Joerg von STUDNITZ
Chargé d'Affaires, a.i.
of the Federal Republic of Germany
to the United Nations

(Signed) Hamilton Whyte
Deputy Permament Representative of the
United Kingdom of Great Britain and
Northern Ireland to the United Nations
Chargé d'Affaires, a.i.

(Signed) William C. Sherman
Acting Permanent Representative
of the United States of America
to the United Nations

Annex C

S/15287
English
Annex
Page 1

Annex

Principles concerning the Constituent Assembly and the Constitution for an independent Namibia

A. Constituent Assembly

1.   In accordance with United Nations Security Council Resolution 435 (1978), elections will be held to select a Constituent Assembly which will adopt a Constitution for an independent Namibia. The Constitution will determine the organization and powers of all levels of government.

- Every adult Namibian will be eligible, without discrimination or fear of intimidation from any source, to vote, campaign and stand for election to the Constituent Assembly.

- Voting will be by secret ballot, with provisions made for those who cannot read or write.

- The date for the beginning of the electoral campaign, the date of elections, the electoral system, the preparation of voters rolls and other aspects of electoral procedures will be promptly decided upon so as to give all political parties and interested persons, without regard to their political views, a full and fair opportunity to organize and participate in the electoral process.

- Full freedom of speech, assembly, movement and press shall be guaranteed.

- The electoral system will seek to ensure fair representation in the Constitutent Assembly to different political parties which gain substantial support in the election.

2.   The Constituent Assembly will formulate the Constitution for an independent Namibia in accordance with the principles in Part B below and will adopt the Constitution as a whole by a two-thirds majority of its total membership.

B.   Principles for a Constitution for an Independent Namibia

1.   Namibia will be a unitary, sovereign and democratic state.

2.   The Constitution will be the supreme law of the state. It may be amended only by a designated process involving the legislature and/or votes cast in a popular referendum.

Annex C

S/15287
English
Annex
Page 2

3.   The Constitution will determine the organization and powers of all levels of government. It will provide for a system of government with three branches: an elected executive branch which will be responsible to the legislative branch; a legislative branch to be elected by universal and equal suffrage which will be responsible for the passage of all laws; and an independent judicial branch which will be responsible for the interpretation of the Constitution and for ensuring its supremacy and the authority of the law. The executive and legislative branches will be constituted by periodic and genuine elections which will be held by secret vote.

4.   The electoral system will be consistent with the principles in A. 1. above.

5.   There will be a declaration of fundamental rights, which will include the rights to life, personal liberty and freedom of movement; to freedom of conscience; to freedom of expression, including freedom of speech and a free press; to freedom of assembly and association, including political parties and trade unions; to due process and equality before the law; to protection from arbitrary deprivation of private property or deprivation of private property without just compensation; and to freedom from racial, ethnic, religious or sexual discrimination. The declaration of rights will be consistent with the provisions of the Universal Declaration of Human Rights. Aggrieved individuals will be entitled to have the courts adjudicate and enforce these rights.

6.   It will be forbidden to create criminal offences with retrospective effect or to provide for increased penalties with retrospective effect.

7.   Provision will be made for the balanced structuring of the public service, the police service and the defense services and for equal access by all to recruitment of these services. The fair administration of personnel policy in relation to these services will be assured by appropriate independent bodies.

8.   Provision will be made for the establishment of elected councils for local and/or regional administration.

**UNITED
NATIONS**

A

General Assembly   Security Council

Distr.
GENERAL

A/44/280 ✓
S/20635
16 May 1989

ORIGINAL: ENGLISH

GENERAL ASSEMBLY
Forty-fourth session
Item 36 of the preliminary list*
QUESTION OF NAMIBIA

SECURITY COUNCIL
Forty-fourth year

<u>Letter dated 15 May 1989 from the Secretary-General to the
President of the Security Council</u>

As you will recall, in my report to the Security Council concerning the
implementation of Security Council resolutions 435 (1978) and 439 (1978) concerning
the question of Namibia (document S/20412 of 23 January 1989), I referred in
paragraph 35 to the fact that the United Nations plan for Namibia includes
agreements and understandings reached by the parties since the adoption of Security
Council resolution 435 (1978) and confirmed as such to me. These agreements and
understandings which, as I stated in my report, remain binding on the parties
include, <u>inter alia</u>, informal understandings reached in 1982 on the question of
impartiality. These understandings, also known as the impartiality package,
include undertakings by the Western Contact Group, the front-line States and
Nigeria and SWAPO, with respect to activities within the United Nations system once
the Security Council meets to authorize the implementation of resolution
435 (1978). The informal understandings also detail corresponding obligations on
the part of the Government of South Africa in order to ensure free and fair
elections in Namibia. As I stated in my report referred to above, at a meeting on
24 September 1982 the representatives of the front-line States and Nigeria, SWAPO
and the Western Contact Group jointly confirmed to me the agreements they had
reached in respect to the impartiality package and presented me with a check-list
of their informal understandings. In separate discussions with the Western Contact
Group, the Government of South Africa also confirmed its agreement to those
understandings which relate to its responsibilities under the plan.

---

*   A/44/50/Rev.1.

89-12649 0989j (E)

/...

Annex D

A/44/280
S/20635
English
Page 2

By resolution 632 (1989), the Security Council approved my report for the implementation of the United Nations plan for Namibia and called upon all parties concerned to honour their commitments to the United Nations plan and to co-operate fully with the Secretary-General in the implementation of that resolution. Under the circumstances I deem it appropriate to bring to your attention and through you to the members of the Security Council the contents of the impartiality package. I am also, by a separate communication, bringing the contents of this letter to the attention of the President of the General Assembly. I am, therefore, arranging for this letter to be issued as both a General Assembly and a Security Council document. The check-list of the informal understandings as presented to me on 24 September 1982 is attached herewith.

(Signed)   Javier PEREZ DE CUELLAR

Annex D

A/44/280
S/20635
English
Page 3

ANNEX

Namibia: Informal check list

1.   The elections will be under the supervision and control of the United Nations (UN) and the UN Special Representative (UNSR) must be satisfied at each stage of that process as to the fairness and appropriateness of all measures affecting the political process at all levels of administration before such measures take effect.

2.   Full freedom of speech, assembly, movement and press shall be guaranteed.

3.   All legislation - including proclamations by the Administrator-General (AG) - that are inconsistent with the plan must be repealed. All discriminatory or restrictive laws, regulations or administrative measures which might abridge or inhibit free and fair elections must be repealed.

4.   The AG must make arrangements for the release, prior to the beginning of the electoral campaign, of all Namibian political prisoners or political detainees held by the South African authorities.

5.   All Namibians in exile shall have the right of peaceful return so that they can participate fully and freely in the elections without risk of arrest, detention, intimidation or imprisonment.

6.   The UN has made provisions to finance the return of these detainees and those in exile ($33 million in original UN budget estimate).

7.   Council of Ministers and National Assembly: UN Security Council resolution (SCR) 439 declares that all unilateral measures taken by the illegal administration in Namibia in relation to the transfer of power are null and void. The December 1978 elections held in Namibia are null and void. No recognition has been accorded either by the UN or any Member State (other than South Africa) to any representatives or organs established by that process. Accordingly only the Administrator-General and UNSR will exercise authority during the transition period within Namibia consistent with the settlement plan and will do so impartially.

8.   Impartiality provisions to be covered by final Security Council enabling resolution: the resolution should emphasize responsibility of all concerned to co-operate to ensure impartial implementation of the settlement plan. The Secretary-General and UN bodies should be directed to act impartially according to the settlement plan and the Secretary-General should be directed to:

        (a) initiate a review of all programmes administered by organs of the UN with respect to Namibia to ensure that they are administered on an impartial basis;

        (b) seek the co-operation of the executive heads of the specialized agencies and other organizations and bodies within the UN system to ensure that their activities with respect to Namibia are conducted impartially.

/...

137

Annex D

A/44/280
S/20635
English
Page 4

9.   At the Security Council meeting to authorize implementation of SCR 435, speakers should be kept to a minimum. Specifically, none of the parties to the election or to the cease-fire would speak.

10. Consideration of the question of Namibia at the regular General Assembly should be suspended during the tran:ition period.

11. The UN will not provide funds for SWAPO or any other party during the transition period.

12. The UN Council for Namibia should refrain from engaging in all public activities once the Security Council meets to authorize implementation.

13. The Commissioner for Namibia and his Office should suspend all political activities during the transition period.

14. SWAPO will voluntarily forego the exercise of the special privileges granted to it by the General Assembly, including participation as an official observer in the General Assembly and in other bodies and conferences within the UN system.

15. Monitoring the South West Africa Police Force: the UN Plan provides that the primary responsibility for maintaining law and order in Namibia during the transition period shall rest with the existing police forces. The AG, to the satisfaction of the UNSR, shall ensure the good conduct of the police forces and shall take the necessary action to ensure their suitability for continued employment during the transition period. The UNSR shall make arrangements when appropriate for UN personnel to accompany the police forces in the discharge of their duties. The police forces would be limited to the carrying of small arms in the normal performance of their duties. The UN Plan also provides that the UNSR will take steps to guarantee against the possibility of intimidation or interference with the electoral process from whatever quarter. The Secretary-General has provided that designated personnel will be at the disposal of the UNSR to ensure that these monitoring responsibilities will be satisfactorily performed. For reasons of safety and effectiveness, these tasks will be performed by civilian personnel who are professionally qualified. The number of UN personnel to monitor the police appropriate to the tasks they are expected to perform will be kept under continuous review.

16. South West Africa Territorial Force (SWATF): The UN Plan specifies that the United Nations Transition Assistance Group (UNTAG) military component will monitor "the demobilization of citizen forces", commandos, and ethnic forces, and the dismantling of their command structure". UNTAG will monitor the demobilization of SWATF and the dismantling of its command structure.

17. Composition of the UNTAG military component will be decided by the Security Council on the recommendation of the Secretary-General after due consultations. Final arrangements for the military component of UNTAG including monitoring of SWAPO facilities in Angola and Zambia will be decided by the Secretary-General, after due consultation.

BASLER AFRIKA BIBLIOGRAPHIEN
Namibia Resource Centre - Southern Africa Library

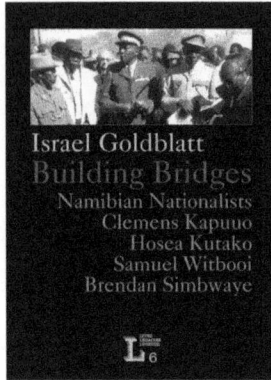

Israel Goldblatt
Building Bridges
Namibian Nationalists Clemens Kapuuo, Hosea Kutako,
Samuel Witbooi, Brendan Simbwaye
Lives Legacies Legends 6
Sept. 2010. Map, ill., index.
CHF 25.00
ISBN 978-3-905758-16-0

Windhoek in the early 60's: The 34-year old politician Clemens Kapuuo knocks at the door of the senior advocate Israel Goldblatt to solicit advice in the developing struggle of Africans against Apartheid. An unusual relationship and friendship, transcending the racial divide in this South African governed territory, develops, lasting for nearly 10 years. Meeting in Goldblatt's chambers or in the Old Location, their consultations soon also include the veteran politicians Chief Hosea Kutako and Kaptein Samuel Witbooi as well as a group of younger nationalist like Rev. Bartholomew Karuaera, Levi Nganjone and Ephraim Vitore. Through Kapuuo, Goldblatt also meets and counsels the long-term prisoner from Caprivi, Brendan Simbwaye.

This book provides the Notes of Israel Goldblatt on the encounters and conversations.

"This was my first meeting with Hosea Kutako. He is about 92. Massive figure – massive personality ... A remarkable man. He took out a cigaret packet while we were discussing and I offered him a cigar. He accepted it and when it went out during the consultation he simply held it unostentatiously. When I noticed it, I lit it for him and he indicated his appreciation. His manners, excellent. No attempt to impose his leadership on me." *Israel Goldblatt on 30 July 1962*

This book and its many photographs pay tribute to Israel Goldblatt and the Namibian nationalists who attempted to build bridges where Apartheid entrenched hatred and racism.

www.baslerafrika.ch

BASLER AFRIKA BIBLIOGRAPHIEN
Namibia Resource Centre - Southern Africa Library

african
posters

Miescher, Giorgio; Henrichsen, Dag (eds.)
African Posters
A Catalogue of the Poster Collection in the Basler Afrika Bibliographien
2004. 301p., ill.
CHF 60.00
ISBN 978-3-905141-82-5

This richly illustrated catalogue presents some 900 full-colour posters from and on Southern Africa, with additions from West and North-Eastern Africa. It provides a representative cross-section of the BAB collection of several thousand African posters, mainly covering the 1970s to the present. The selection reveals the significance of posters in everyday African life as well as for historical research. The catalogue is envisaged as a reference work, and each illustrated poster is provided with available bibliographic data.

The opening essay of the catalogue offers an introduction to posters as part of a visual history of Africa. This is followed by eight chapters (each with an introductory text) in which posters are grouped and considered thematically. The topics are:

liberation movements and exile • solidarity and Anti-Apartheid • elections • nation building • awareness and health • economy • knowledge, information, belief• leisure and pleasure

"On the one hand, the posters reproduced here could be used to expand on the history of the liberation and solidarity movements … On the other hand, they illustrate the way in which politics inspired art … This is a lovely book, produced with great care."
William Beinart in *Journal of Southern African Studies*

www.baslerafrika.ch

www.ingramcontent.com/pod-product-compliance
Lightning Source LLC
Chambersburg PA
CBHW032102080426
42733CB00006B/377